GCSE
ENGLISH
LITERATURE
for
OCR

D. C. Coleman
Chief Examiner

Annie Fox

Garrett O'Doherty

Angela Topping

Carmel Waldron

OCR
RECOGNISING ACHIEVEMENT
OXFORD
UNIVERSITY PRESS
Official Publisher Partnership

Contents

Unit 3: Prose from Different Cultures

Unit 4: Literary Heritage Prose and Contemporary Poetry

How to Use This Book

Welcome to your GCSE English Literature course!

The aim of this book is to prepare you for the OCR GCSE English Literature examinations and Controlled Assessments. It has been written in consultation with OCR by a chief examiner and several practising teachers and Teachit contributors. This means that you will not only find plenty of fun and engaging activities to build your skills and knowledge, but also all the help and advice you need to tackle your assessments.

This book includes a range of useful **features**.

- **How to approach** sections outline the requirements of each part of the specification.
- **Preparing for** sections offer invaluable guidance on preparing for exams and Controlled Assessments to help you achieve your best results.
- **Learning checklists** at the start of each chapter help to explain the Assessment Objectives and tell you what skills will be covered in the pages that follow.
- **Functional Skills** boxes provide real-life application of your GCSE knowledge, helping to prepare you for the stand-alone Functional Skills assessments.
- **Examiner's tips** boxes contain useful advice from a real examiner.
- **Exam-style questions** and sample Controlled Assessment tasks modelled on real papers help you to practise and feel more confident.
- **Sample student responses** show examples of high- and low-scoring answers with detailed Examiner's comments to help you develop and improve your own work.
- **Try This!** pages give you a chance to take a break from the specification requirements and get to grips with English Literature in a fun and creative way.

The book is organized according to the OCR GCSE English Literature specification, which is made up of four units:

- Unit 1: Literary Heritage Linked Texts
- Unit 2: Modern Drama
- Unit 3: Prose from Different Cultures
- Unit 4: Literary Heritage Prose and Contemporary Poetry.

Each of these units is assessed using different **Assessment Objectives**, and the chapters in this book help you to learn what is expected from you for each objective.

The four Assessment Objectives (AOs) for English Literature are:

AO1

Respond to texts critically and imaginatively; select and evaluate relevant textual detail to illustrate and support interpretations.

AO2

Explain how language, structure and form contribute to writers' presentation of ideas, themes and settings.

AO3

Make comparisons and explain links between texts, evaluating writers' different ways of expressing meaning and achieving effects.

AO4

Relate texts to their social, cultural and historical contexts; explain how texts have been influential and significant to self and other readers in different contexts and at different times.

Unit 1

Literary Heritage Linked Texts

HOW TO APPROACH UNIT 1

What will be in the assessment?

Unit 1 consists of **two** parts:
- Shakespeare and Film/Audio/Live performance
- Literary Heritage Poetry

The whole unit is worth 25% of the English Literature GCSE.

How will this unit be assessed?

Unit 1 is tested through **Controlled Assessment**. This means that you will write **two extended essays**, one about a Shakespeare play and the other about two linked poems by the same poet.

The tasks are set by the exam board and they change each year. They will be released in June, ready for the assessment in the following January and June, so you will have plenty of time to think about them, discuss them in the classroom and do some research before you write anything. Your teacher will offer advice and guidance as usual.

What are controlled conditions?

When you write your final response to each task, you will do so under controlled conditions. This means that your work will be closely supervised; you will not be able to communicate with other students or obtain help from your teacher. You will need more than one writing session to complete your response, so you must hand in what you have written at the end of each session; it will then be given back to you at the start of the next session.

Can I take notes into the assessment?

You can have notes with you when you work on your final version – however, this does not mean you can take in a draft of your essay! It would be wise to keep your notes in an orderly form, organized on a sheet of A4, rather than attempting to work with a huge stack of paper on your desk.

What play will I study?

You will study the written form of **one** of the following plays together with a film verision, an audio version or a live performance of the same play:

- *Julius Caesar*
- *The Merchant of Venice*
- *Macbeth*
- *Romeo & Juliet.*

Your teacher will choose which play as well as which film, audio or live version to watch or listen to.

What will the task be?

There will be **one** task set on the play chosen. This will require you to comment on and analyse aspects of the play linked to a scene or scenes from the film or live version. You will know what the task is months in advance of the assessment, so you will have time to get to know the play well, along with the scene or scenes you will be analysing.

How will the task be marked?

This task will be marked against the Assessment Objectives listed below.

- **AO1: Respond to texts critically and imaginatively; select and evaluate relevant textual detail to illustrate and support interpretations.**

  This means that you need to show how you interpret the text, using close reference to the words to explain your ideas.

- **AO3: Make comparisons and explain links between texts, evaluating writers' different ways of expressing meaning and achieving effects.**

  This objective tests your ability to identify similarities and differences between the written version of the play and a film version, audio version or live performance

The quality of your writing will also be assessed. This means you need to:

- ensure that your writing is legible and that your spelling, punctuation and grammar are accurate so that meaning is clear
- present information in a form that suits its purpose
- use a suitable structure and style of writing.

EXAMINER'S TIPS

Although you will not be writing on the whole play in your assessment, you

Responding to a Shakespeare Text

LEARNING CHECKLIST

In this chapter you will learn to:

1 Respond with insight and imagination; select text detail to support interpretations.

AO1

Why is Shakespeare still studied and performed?

Although William Shakespeare (1564–1616) lived and wrote hundreds of years ago, his plays are still performed and studied around the world. Actors compete to perform his most famous roles and theatre companies devote themselves to staging his plays. Why?

ACTIVITY I

a Read the thoughts of some students below and rank their ideas in order of how strongly you agree with them.

1 He wrote exciting plays with great plots and memorable characters.

2 He's the greatest writer of all time. Everyone should be familiar with at least one of his plays.

3 His plays deal with universal themes like love, death, friendship and revenge.

4 His plays are challenging, so it's an accomplishment if you understand them!

b Now write your own paragraph explaining why you think Shakespeare is still studied and performed.

What is interpretation?

An **interpretation** is a point of view about the meaning and intention of a text. Shakespeare's plays are open to many interpretations, which often reflect the period in which they are being performed. A director may interpret a play by:

- emphasizing a key theme, such as war or prejudice
- adapting the setting to a certain era to make it more relevant or dramatic
- choosing actors who represent qualities that the director wishes to emphasize, such as youth, beauty or danger.

When reading your Shakespeare play think about how you would interpret it to make it interesting and meaningful to an audience.

ACTIVITY 4

In a small group, improvise a day-time talk show programme in which the characters from the Shakespeare play you are studying meet with a counsellor to discuss and attempt to solve their problems. Use your knowledge of the play to role-play a character of your choice as believably as possible. One person from the group will need to play the part of the talk show host. The host should keep the discussion on topic and bring it to a resolution at the end.

ACTIVITY 5

In role as one of the characters from the Shakespeare play you are studying, write a letter to an agony aunt from a magazine explaining a dilemma or anxiety that you have. Swap your letter with a partner and write a reply to your partner's letter in role as the agony aunt. Some ideas are given below.

PORTIA
Does he only want me for my money?

JULIET
I love my father, but I love Romeo more!

BRUTUS
Should I betray a friend to be true to my beliefs?

SHYLOCK
She has humiliated me!

ANTONIO
He'd rather spend time with his friends than hang out with me.

MACBETH
Is it ever wrong to be ambitious?

MACDUFF
I suspect my friend of murder!

SHAKESPEARE AND FILM/AUDIO/LIVE PERFORMANCE

Do I need to read the whole play?

At first sight, it might seem like it will save time to read only those parts of the play referred to in the task. Time-saving it certainly would be, but, if you don't know the whole play, you're certain to trip up somewhere in your response. It would be like writing about the first 20 minutes of a football game in which the home team scores twice; if you don't know that they then went on to lose 2-4, your analysis is going to look very limited. So read and watch/listen to the whole play.

Should I focus on a particular scene?

The task will ask you to refer closely to a specified scene or scenes so it is important that you are very familiar with them. This means that you should take extra care to understand the details of the vocabulary, the stage directions, the characters and the events that occur within the scene(s).

What should I look for when reading the play?

When reading the play, try to imagine that you are a director. Consider:

- what happens in the specified scene or scenes
- the words, actions and intentions of the characters
- how the actors say their lines and what they should be emphasizing
- how and where the actors move
- where each scene is set
- the costumes
- the lighting.

Focus on anything that brings out the drama of the scene or scenes. Discuss your ideas with your teacher and others in your class. If there is time to do it, you could direct your own version.

HOW TO APPROACH UNIT 1

LITERARY HERITAGE POETRY

What do I need to study?

For this part of Unit 1 you will study **either** 15 poems by one poet chosen from the following:

- Robert Browning
- Christina Rossetti
- Thomas Hardy
- William Shakespeare
- Wilfred Owen

or you will study Chaucer's *The General Prologue to the Canterbury Tales*. All of these texts can be found in your Anthology.

What will the tasks be like?

Two tasks will be set on each poet and you must respond to **one** of those tasks. The task will ask you to compare two linked, named poems by the poet you have studied. It will contain a list of bullet points, suggesting areas that you should consider in your response.

How much should I write?

For this part of the unit, you will write an extended essay of up to **1000 words** and you will have about **three hours** to complete your writing. This writing time is likely to be split across a number of shorter sessions.

How will my response be marked?

For this task you will be marked on the Assessment Objectives listed below.

- **AO1: Respond to texts critically and imaginatively; select and evaluate relevant textual detail to illustrate and support interpretations.**
  This tests your ability to interpret the texts and convey your own ideas. Personal interpretations are valid as long as you can back up your ideas with evidence from the text.

- **AO3: Make comparisons and explain links between texts, evaluating writers' different ways of expressing meaning and achieving effects.**
  This means that you need to find connections between the two poems and explore them. The connections might include similarities and differences in theme, style, viewpoint and structure.

EXAMINER'S TIPS

When deciding which task to respond to, look carefully at the wording of the task, as well as the poems specified. Try to weigh up which task you feel you can respond to most thoroughly before choosing which one to attempt.

Responding to Poetry

LEARNING CHECKLIST

In this chapter you will learn to:

1 Respond with insight and imagination; select text detail to support interpretations.

AO1

Why poets use literary devices

Literary devices are the tools of the poet's trade. They enable the poet to communicate effectively with the reader. Poets use literary devices to:

- help us **see** images in our minds, through simile, metaphor, personification and symbolism
- help us **hear** the feeling in the poems through onomatopoeia, alliteration, assonance, consonance and rhyme
- shape ideas into **patterns** by using rhythm, rhyme, repetition and set structures.

Poets select words and phrases carefully to prompt specific emotions and create very precise effects.

Literary devices are an integral part of the poet's creative process; they are not just thrown in afterwards. When writing about poems, you need to think carefully about the literary devices used, why the poet has used them and the effects they create.

ACTIVITY I

Remind yourself of the meanings of different literary devices by putting them into a diagram. Decide how best to present your ideas visually: you might choose a spider diagram similar to the one shown here; a tree with different branches or a 'washing line' device. Use underlining to highlight key terms, and then write definitions and give examples. It might be helpful to group the terms together in different categories, such as 'comparisons'.

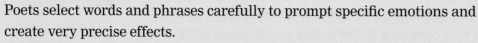

personification: giving something <u>living</u> qualities, e.g. the wind whispered

LITERARY DEVICES

Comparing how characters are presented

In *The Canterbury Tales*, Geoffrey Chaucer wrote about a group of pilgrims travelling to a shrine at Canterbury Cathedral. The tales were written over 600 years ago but Chaucer gives his characters such realistic, timeless qualities that we can imagine them as people we might meet today.

Think carefully about the Wife of Bath and the Miller from 'The General Prologue to The Canterbury Tales'. With a partner, discuss which famous living people have similar qualities to these characters. Then try the activities below.

ACTIVITY 2

a Using two separate sheets of paper, make a sketch of each character. Make sure you draw what is described in the text.
  - Annotate your drawings with words and phrases from the text.
  - Explain what each description tells us about the character. Many physical descriptions give clues about personality, values and status. What do these descriptions suggest?

b Compare the ways Chaucer portrays these characters.
  - Are there similarities in the way Chaucer makes you feel about them?
  - Are there similarities in terms of the language he uses to describe them?

ACTIVITY 3

Imagine these two characters are well known to the general public today. Write a short article about one of them for a celebrity gossip magazine. For example, perhaps the Wife of Bath has been seen out with a celebrity billionaire or the Miller, a famous wrestler, has caused a brawl at a local nightspot. Include a brief interview or comment from the character in your article.

Remember to base the personality of your chosen character on details from the poem.

Comparing the feelings described

Although the situations described may be very different, poems can be linked by the feelings or emotions that a writer expresses. In the poems 'The Darkling Thrush' and 'Beeny Cliff', Thomas Hardy expresses feelings that swing between sadness and depression, and joy and optimism. One poem is about hearing a thrush in winter and the other is about his dead love.

ACTIVITY 4

Copy and complete the grids below to help you compare the poems. You can find both texts in your Anthology.

First, select phrases from 'The Darkling Thrush' that show the feelings listed in the grid below.

FEELINGS	QUOTATIONS
depression	
loneliness	
joy	
optimism	

Then, consider the quotations from 'Beeny Cliff' in the second grid and write down the feelings that you think they suggest.

QUOTATIONS	FEELINGS
'...with bright hair flapping free –'	
'The woman whom I loved so'	
'The woman now is – elsewhere –'	
'...and will laugh there nevermore.'	

ACTIVITY 5

Choose one of the two poems from Activity 4. Design two masks showing the feelings expressed in this poem. The first mask should represent the feelings conveyed at the beginning of the poem and the second should show the feelings expressed at end.

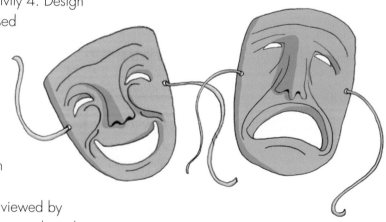

- Decorate the masks with suitable words and phrases from your chosen text.
- Imagine you are the poet being interviewed by a student. Explain why you used these words and phrases in the poem.

Comparing situations

Even when a poet is writing about similar situations, the effects created by separate poems can be very different. Two of Browning's poems are linked by their common situation: a girl is dead and a man speaks of his love for her. The feelings expressed in both poems are powerful, but they are different in that one is a pure, spiritual feeling and the other a violent and sexual passion.

In 'Evelyn Hope', Evelyn, a 16-year-old girl, has died and the narrator, a man three times her age, visits her bedside, confesses his love, and imagines the two of them together in a future life. In 'Porphyria's Lover' a poor man is visited by his lover, Porphyria, who is upper-class and wealthy. The narrator knows Porphyria will not give up her lifestyle even though she is in love. At a moment of pure happiness, he strangles her, so she will never leave him.

ACTIVITY 6

Choose one of the poems mentioned above and read it in your Anthology.
a Write a short playscript where the two people from your chosen poem meet in an imaginary afterlife. What would they say to each other?
b Rewrite the playscript as a monologue in modern English, to be spoken by the narrator.

ACTIVITY 7

a For each poem, create a spider diagram like the one on the right, adding other boxes if needed. Add notes to the diagram about:
- the way the situation develops in each poem
- the way each woman is portrayed
- how the poet reveals the motives of each man
- what the man's feelings are in each poem.

b How are the situations that the poet writes about in 'Evelyn Hope' and 'Porphyria's Lover' similar and different? Use your completed spider diagrams to help you structure your answer.

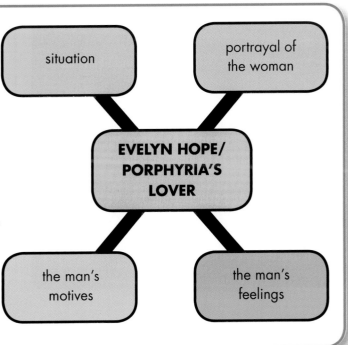

situation

portrayal of the woman

EVELYN HOPE/ PORPHYRIA'S LOVER

the man's motives

the man's feelings

Comparing the use of language

The way that a writer uses language can give him or her an individual style, so that even when writing about different subjects, this style is recognizable. For example, Christina Rossetti uses language that is simple, with few long words. Using this apparently simple language, however, she is able to express profound ideas which might otherwise be obscured by complicated phrases.

Look at 'In the Willow Shade' and 'Cousin Kate' in your Anthology. Use the list of language features below to help you complete the activities on this page.

Language features

- **alliteration** – words that begin with the same sound: 'brittle branches'
- **assonance** – words with similar vowel sounds: 'faded shapes'
- **consonance** – words with similar consonant sounds: 'happy appeal'
- **rhyme** – words with matching end sounds: 'sing/ring' (end rhymes appear at the end of separate lines; internal rhymes appear within the same line)
- **onomatopoeia** – words that sound like what they describe: 'clatter and clunk'
- **repetition**
- **imagery**
- **metaphor** – a comparison where one thing is actually said to be another: 'she is my sunshine'
- **simile** – a comparison using 'like' or 'as': 'he looks like a frog'
- **contrast** – a comparison of different ideas: 'I fell as they advanced'

ACTIVITY 8

Using copies of 'In the Willow Shade' and 'Cousin Kate':

- highlight examples of language features used in the poems
- with a partner, discuss **why** these techniques are used in each poem and what effects they have on the reader.

ACTIVITY 9

Write four short paragraphs comparing the writer's use of language in both poems. Think about:

- how the poems sound through the use of rhyme, rhythm and sound patterning
- the pictures the writer creates in your head by using imagery and engaing your senses
- how the language helps to reveal feelings in the poems; for example, the use of the word 'solaced' in the first stanza of 'In the Willow Shade'
- your own personal response to the language.

Writing comparisons

This chapter has shown you how to make links between two poems by the same author; for example, where characters or situations may be different but the language and feelings are similar, or where the language and feelings are different but the subject matter is related.

Now practise linking two poems by the writer you are studying by completing the activities on this page.

ACTIVITY 10

Work with a partner or in a small group.

a Choose two of your set poems from the Anthology. Using copies of the poems, place them side by side.

b Discuss whether you think the poems are linked by subject matter, situation, character, feelings or language – or more than one of these.

c Highlight all the words and phrases that reveal links between the two poems. Use a different colour to highlight words and phrases that reveal differences between them.

ACTIVITY 11

a Copy and complete the grid below to examine one similarity and one difference between the two poems, with supporting evidence.

b Repeat the grid to consider further similarities and differences in the poems. If you have time, try to complete three grids on the same texts.

POINTS TO COMPARE	POEM 1	POEM 2
identify a <u>similarity</u>		
find one quotation from each poem as evidence		
find a second quotation from each poem as evidence		
explain what the quotations reveal		
identify a <u>difference</u>		
find one quotation from each poem as evidence		
find a second quotation from each poem as evidence		
explain what the quotations reveal		

c The grids could then form the basic structure of an assessment task. Alternatively, you could begin by analysing one poem in detail at first, then go through the second poem, indicating similarities and differences. Whichever method of comparison you choose, ensure you back up your points with evidence from the texts.

EXAMINER'S TIPS

OCR RECOGNISING ACHIEVEMENT

Remember, when discussing the language techniques, you don't need to give definitions of these techniques. The examiner already knows what alliteration is; he or she is looking for your explanation of how specific examples are effective within the poem.

LITERARY HERITAGE POETRY

How many poems should I read?

Even though you will know well in advance which two poems you will be comparing, it is sensible to read all 15 poems by your chosen poet, or in the case of Chaucer, the whole of *The General Prologue to the Canterbury Tales*, in your Anthology. This will help you to develop your understanding of the poet's favoured style, themes and his or her subject matter.

Can I discuss the task in class?

When you actually write your response to the task, you must work independently. Before you write it, however, you can think about the task, discuss it in class and make notes on it. You can check websites and read up on it in libraries. Your teacher will give you advice about where to find information.

What is meant by 'compare'?

The instruction 'compare' means that you need to pick out features that the two poems have in common and also focus on interesting differences between them.

UNIT 1

How should I plan my response?

Before writing, you should plan out the structure of your response. You can approach the task in a number of ways, so use the approach that suits you best. The plan below provides one possible structure.

Introduction
- Give a brief overview of the two poems saying what they are about.
- Suggest how the poems are similar or how they are different.

Part 1
- Discuss the first poem in detail.
- Refer closely to the language of the first poem.

Part 2
- Discuss the second poem in detail, referring back to the first poem to compare.
- Refer closely to the language of the second poem, referring back to the first poem to compare.

Conclusion
- Bring both poems together, highlighting their key similarities and differences.

Can I take the poems into the assessment?

Yes, you may take **unannotated** or 'clean' copies of the poems into the Controlled Assessment with you. This means you are **not** allowed to write in the margins of this material during your preparation for the task.

EXAMINER'S TIPS

An alternative approach to writing your response is to switch continually from one poem to the other. This approach can help you to make a closer and more fluid comparison but unless you structure your work clearly, there is a risk that your argument could appear scattered or muddled.

SAMPLE TASKS

LITERARY HERITAGE POETRY

Shakespeare's Sonnets

Poems: *Sonnet 18* and *Sonnet 19*

Compare the ways in which Shakespeare portrays the passage of time and its effects in these sonnets.

You should consider:

- the situations Shakespeare describes
- the feelings he portrays
- the language he uses.

Student response 1.3 (extract from opening)

These two sonnets are from Shakespeare's sequence of one hundred and fifty-four sonnets. Sonnets are fourteen-line poems usually about love, as these two are. They are also about the way time changes things. It can bring about death where people wander in Death's shade as in Sonnet 18, or old age as in Sonnet 19, where a personified Time draws lines on 'fair brows' with his 'antique pen'. Both sonnets are similar as they make clear in the last lines that poetry can outlast both death and time.

Sonnet 18 begins with a question probably to the person the writer loves. We do not know who this person is. It might be a woman, the Dark Lady of the Sonnets, or a man. In line eleven of Sonnet 19, for example, a man is clearly indicated: 'Him in thy course untainted do allow'. The person could also be a

a good quick overview and a relevant reference to form

valid comment on structure

apt quotations embedded fluently into the student's writing

good comparison

Student response I.3 (extract from opening) continued

made-up lover if Shakespeare is, as some think, using these sonnets to develop his skills as a poet.

evidence of research

The question shows the poet is uncertain about the comparison, but he is able to introduce the theme of nature, which runs through most of the poem. Comparing his lover to a summer's day, he thinks, does not do her justice. She is 'more lovely' and 'more temperate'. A summer's day can produce rough winds or the sun can be too hot.

good detail to begin paragraph

He also says that summer does not last long; its 'lease' or contract with a landlord is short, but he says in line 9 that his lover's 'summer' is 'eternal', another reason for rejecting the comparison with her to a summer's day. I think that when Shakespeare writes that his lover shall 'Not lose possession of that fair thou ow'st' he is extending the landlord metaphor. The lover owns her beauty and hasn't just rented it short-term.

an imaginative and well-founded interpretation

good awareness of sonnet structure

For living people, Time ends with death, but Shakespeare says that the lover will live forever in his eternal lines. His proof comes in the couplet that follows his four quatrains, where he confidently states that his lover will live forever, or as long at least as the human race continues:

'So long as men can breathe or eyes can see,
So long lives this, and this gives life to thee.'

suitable quotation

In Sonnet 18 Time brings about change and death, in Sonnet 19 it brings old age. In both sonnets Time brings something that nobody really wants. Sonnet 18 opens with the poet asking his lover a question. In contrast Sonnet 19 opens with the poet addressing Time directly, so Time has been personified as if it's a monster guilty of 'heinous' or particularly horrible crimes.

good comparison

excellent contrast and imaginative response

Student response 1.3 (extract from opening) continued

Where Shakespeare used the season of summer in Sonnet 18 to show the effects of time, he uses animals in the first four lines of Sonnet 19. He describes how time blunts the lion's paws and plucks 'the keen teeth from the fierce tiger's jaws'. Like Sonnet 18, Sonnet 19 refers to the seasons. An interesting word here is 'fleet'st' which means that Time is hurrying.

Just like Sonnet 18, Sonnet 19 says that poetry can beat Time: 'My love shall in my verse ever live young'. The key word in this line is 'ever'. Even if Shakespeare's lover gets old, the lover will always be young in the sonnet.

I found the last couplet interesting because Shakespeare seems to challenge 'old Time' by saying 'do thy worst' and I think the irregular rhythm of the last line helps to convey this tone. In the sonnet the rhythm is iambic, with an unstressed syllable followed by a stressed syllable. In the last three words of Sonnet 19 the stress appears to fall on the last syllable of 'ever' and on the last word 'young'. Therefore, Shakespeare emphasizes triumph over Time.

good linking of texts

effective reference to the poet's tone

confident use of technical terms

effectively picks out specific words

close, tight comparison

good critical response to technique

EXAMINER'S COMMENTS OCR

- The analysis of Sonnet 18 is perceptive and well supported and the student has responded imaginatively to the poem.

- The student moves smoothly on to Sonnet 19 and effectively starts to compare and contrast.

- An excellent, thorough and perceptive response that would achieve a top-band mark.

Sample task I.4

Wilfred Owen

EITHER

Task 1

Poems: *Dulce et Decorum Est* and *The Sentry*

Compare how Wilfred Owen portrays the suffering of men in war in these poems.

You should consider:

- the situations Owen describes
- the feelings he portrays
- the language he uses.

OR

Task 2

Poems: *Exposure* and *Futility*

Compare the way Owen presents nature in these poems.

You should consider:

- the situations Owen describes
- the feelings he portrays
- the language he uses.

EXAMINER'S TIPS

Remember, your teacher will collect your work in and lock it away at the end of each assessment session, and will return it to you at the start of the next one. Your teacher will decide how many sessions you will have, but in total you will have **three hours** of Controlled Assessment time to write your final response to each task.

Unit 2

Modern Drama

HOW TO APPROACH UNIT 2

What will be in this assessment?

Unit 2 focuses on the study of one modern play chosen from a list of six:

- *The History Boys* by Alan Bennett
- *Hobson's Choice* by Harold Brighouse
- *A View from the Bridge* by Arthur Miller
- *An Inspector Calls* by J.B. Priestley
- *Educating Rita* by Willy Russell
- *Journey's End* by R. C. Sherriff.

How will I be assessed?

This unit will be tested by an exam that will last **45 minutes**. In the exam, you must answer **one** question on the play you have studied, from a choice of two.

The first question will be passage-based. The second question will be more general and will require comment, criticism and analysis.

If you sit a Foundation tier paper, your answer will be marked out of **27**. All passage-based questions on the Foundation tier paper will include bullet-point prompts to suggest what you should cover in your answer. Higher tier questions do not feature prompts and answers are marked out of **40**. Whichever tier you sit, Unit 2 is worth 25% of your English Literature GCSE.

What should I focus on in my response?

In the exam, you will need to show that you understand what drama involves. There will often be conflict between characters, such as Mr Birling and Inspector Goole in *An Inspector Calls*. Sometimes characters experience conflict within themselves, such as Hibbert in *Journey's End,* or a character might experience conflict within his or her community, like Eddie Carbone in *A View from the Bridge.*

Drama also directly involves the audience, so you should always try to think about how an audience might respond to the lines you read. Would they be amused, horrified, puzzled, gripped or react in some other way? Drama often involves characters who evolve with the plot. Some questions may therefore ask you to look at the ways characters, like Rita in *Educating Rita* or Willie Mossop in *Hobson's Choice,* develop as the play progresses.

How will my work be marked?

You will marked according to the Assessment Objectives listed below.

- **AO1: Respond to texts critically and imaginatively; select and evaluate relevant textual detail to illustrate and support interpretations.**
  This means you need to make a clear personal response to the text and use relevant quotations to back up your points.
- **AO2: Explain how language, structure and form contribute to writers' presentation of ideas, themes and settings.**
  This means that you need to comment on and analyse the language features, structure and form that the writer has used and be able to explain the effects these have on the reader.

EXAMINER'S TIPS

- ✔ One of the best ways to enhance your drama studies is to **see** as much drama as you can. Ideally, you should watch plays on stage, but if that is not possible there is plenty of drama on TV to discuss and analyse.
- ✔ Passage-based questions on drama will usually ask you to discuss what is **dramatic** about the passage.

LEARNING CHECKLIST

In this chapter you will learn to:

1 Respond with insight and imagination; select text detail to support interpretations.

2 Explain how the writer uses language, structure and form to present ideas, themes and settings.

Approaching a passage-based question

In your exam you may choose to answer a passage-based question. This means that the question refers very specifically to an extract of the play that is printed in the exam booklet. When answering this type of question you will need a thorough knowledge of the whole play, but most of your answer should be focused on what is contained within the passage.

When approaching a passage-based question:

1 Read the question first.

2 Read the passage closely, at least twice, thinking carefully about the following points, and making notes if necessary:

- what happens before and after this extract
- who's on stage
- the relationships between the characters, and how they behave and talk
- relevant themes
- the tone
- any interesting language used
- the use of stage directions.

3 Read the question again and think carefully about exactly what you are being asked to do. It may help to annotate the question, as shown in the example on the right:

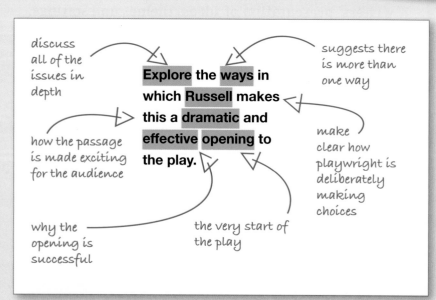

discuss all of the issues in depth

Explore the ways in which Russell makes this a dramatic and effective opening to the play.

suggests there is more than one way

how the passage is made exciting for the audience

make clear how playwright is deliberately making choices

why the opening is successful

the very start of the play

UNIT 2

Read the extract below from *Educating Rita* where Rita, a working-class hairdresser and adult student, explains why she could not attend a dinner party hosted by her university tutor, Frank. She explains how she feels divided between two worlds: her working-class background and the new middle-class world of her education.

From *Educating Rita*
by Willy Russell

Rita

I'm all right with you, here in this room; but when I saw those people you were with I couldn't come in. I would have seized up. Because I'm a freak. I can't talk to the people I live with any more. An' I can't talk to the likes of them on Saturday, or them out there, because I can't learn the language. I'm a half-caste. I went back to the pub where Denny was, an' me mother, an' our Sandra, an' her mates. I'd decided I wasn't comin' here again.

ACTIVITY 7

a With a partner, discuss what we learn about Rita from the language she uses in this extract. Consider:
- her style of speech; for example, colloquial style, choice of vocabulary and abbreviations
- what she says; for example, describing what happened on Saturday
- how she expresses her feelings and how she describes herself
- her current situation.

b Now write a paragraph to explain your interpretation of Rita in this passage. Focus on the language she uses and remember to refer closely to the text to back up your points.
You may find the words in the panels helpful to use in your answer.

working class   limbo

terrified   inferior

safe   repetition

suggests   reinforces

frustrated   represents   alienated   colloquial   isolated

adjective   abbreviation   communication   racial terminology   middle class

TRY THIS!

...place

Characters online

How do you think the key characters from the play you are studying would portray themselves online? The activities below require you to imagine and then put this into practice – see how creative you can be!

ACTIVITY 1

Create a webpage on a social networking site for one of the main characters in your chosen play. Think about:

- the details that would go in his or her profile
- who might be on his or her friends list
- which other characters might leave messages for your character and what they would say.

Dislikes:

Dreams:

Fears:

My
frie...

ACTIVITY 2

Imagine that one of the key characters from the play you have been studying has been using a social networking site, such as Twitter to tell friends about his or her experiences. Create 14 short messages ('tweets') to trace his or her development across the play. These should inform others about what the character is doing and how he or she feels about events and other characters. Make it clear how the character changes and develops.

ACTIVITY 3

Find an example of a dating page, either online or in your local newspaper, where single people advertise for a companion or partner. They often use abbreviations, such as GSOH, LTR and WLTM to save space. Research what these abbreviations mean. Then pick two characters from your chosen play and write an online entry for both. Try to make them as funny as you can!

Romeo Montague

Juliet is the most beautiful girl i have ever seen :)

4 minutes ago

Benvolio & I are going out toni...

4 minutes ago

Mum & Dad are arguing...

4 minutes a...

Name: Romeo Montague

Location: Verona, Italy

20
following

55
followers

Following

TV links

The following activities make links between your chosen play and different TV programmes. They will help you to consolidate your understanding of the key characters in the play you are studying.

ACTIVITY 4

Blackadder Goes Forth is a famous comedy series starring Rowan Atkinson. Watch Episode 6 (the final one) of the series.

- Do you see any similarity between the comic characters in this episode and the characters in *Journey's End*?
- How are the soldiers' attitudes to the war and the use of language similar in both?
- How is the action similar?
- Do you think the play could have been the inspiration for the show?

ACTIVITY 5

Crimewatch is television programme designed to help the police catch criminals. It uses reconstructions to help jog the public's memory about particular crimes. The programme follows a very formulaic approach. Watch an episode of it and make notes about:

- the presenters
- the running order of things
- how interviews are carried out
- the way reconstructions are staged and described.

Identify a major incident that occurs in the play you are studying, and in a group of no more than six, script, perform and film your own reconstruction of the events that lead up to it. For example, it could be the killing of Eddie by Marco in *A View from the Bridge*; Irwin's accident in *The History Boys* or the series of events leading up to the death of Eva Smith in *An Inspector Calls*.

LEARNING CHECKLIST

In this chapter you will learn to:

1 Respond with insight and imagination; select text detail to support interpretations.

2 Explain how the writer uses language, structure and form to present ideas, themes and settings.

Understanding the significance of characters

In your exam, you may choose to answer a general question on the play you are studying, rather than one that is based on a set passage. Whichever type of question you answer, you will be expected to show the ability to read with insight, to support your points with relevant quotations and to discuss how ideas are reinforced through the use of language, structure and form.

If you decide to answer a general question on the play, you will need to show a clear understanding of the entire play and in particular, demonstrate a good understanding of the characters. You will also need to show the examiner that you appreciate how the playwright creates and uses characters to represent particular points of view.

Look at the opening and closing lines of an extract from *A View from the Bridge* printed on the right. This extract was taken from Act One. Turn to your copy of the play to read the extract in full. In this extract, Alfieri, a lawyer from New York, reveals his thoughts to the audience.

From *A View from the Bridge*
by Arthur Miller

Opening line

[…]who have I dealt with in my life? Longshoremen and their wives […]

Closing line

[…] and sat there as powerless as I, and watched it run its bloody course.

After you have chosen a suitable quotation to support your point, try to get into the habit of examining the quotation in more detail in your answer. Think of it as using the quotation as a springboard to develop a further, deeper insight into the text.

ACTIVITY 6

The table below focuses on Mr Birling. Complete the table by selecting an appropriate supporting quotation for the point given or providing further comment and analysis. The first row has been completed as an example.

POINT	QUOTATION	COMMENT/ANALYSIS
Mistaken in his views	'a few German officers talking nonsense'	Reads the political situation completely wrong which calls his judgement into question.
Patronizing	'You've a lot to learn yet.'	
Egotistical		Feels his status as a businessman makes him important.
Likes the sound of his own voice		Repeating himself suggests he likes taking centre stage.
Racist	'Russia [...] will always be behindhand'	

ACTIVITY 7

Now write an analysis of how the playwright portrays Mr Birling in an unsympathetic way. Bear in mind that in an exam you would also need to analyse how his character is portrayed elsewhere in the play.

ACTIVITY 8

Choose a key character from the play you are studying and analyse at least two of his or her speeches at different points in the play. Explore how the playwright portrays the character. You may find it helpful to use a grid like the one in Activity 6 above.

How can I prepare for this exam?

The best form of preparation is to make sure that you know the play well. Even when you feel familiar with the play as a whole, it is a good idea to re-read parts of it from time to time to refresh your memory.

You should always bear in mind, however, that the play you are studying was written to be acted out in front of an audience and not simply read as you might read a novel. As you read, try to think about how the play might work on stage, how the actors might speak, how they might move and how this would affect the audience.

Should I watch film versions of the play?

There are good film versions of most of these plays. However, while these are useful, you should use them with care because some do not always stick closely to the original script. For example, the character Denny who features in the 1983 film version of *Educating Rita* does not appear in Willy Russell's original play. Also, remember that in this unit, you should write about the set text only and not a film or audio version.

What will the passage-based questions be like?

The passage-based question will almost certainly ask you to identify what is particularly **dramatic** about the extract you have been given, so it's important to have thought clearly about what you think the term 'dramatic' means.

Passage-based questions may also be focused on your reaction to the text as a member of an audience. For example, you may be asked what you find amusing, disturbing, entertaining or moving.

EXAMINER'S TIPS

- ✔ Remember that the examiner is not setting a trick question. He or she is expecting you to respond to the passage exactly as the question suggests.
- ✔ If you are asked to specify and discuss what you think is dramatic about a passage, think about what makes it particularly exciting, shocking, moving or emotionally intense. Think about what impact certain lines would have on the audience.

What should I keep in mind when answering passage-based questions?

When you respond to questions on drama texts remember to look carefully at the **stage directions** as well as at what the characters say. Writers will often give precise instructions about what actors should do and guidance about how they should deliver their lines. Some playwrights, like Arthur Miller in *A View from the Bridge*, include direction about the design of the set.

Passage-based questions require you to focus most of your response on the passage provided. It may be appropriate to refer, briefly, to the wider play but you should not get side-tracked and should always aim to bring your answer back to the words and features of the extract.

What will the general questions be like?

General questions may ask you to consider the importance and significance of a particular character's role in the play; for example, the role of Hibbert in Journey's End. When considering how 'significant' a character is, you should think about what he or she reveals or represents in the play. Remember that this type of question is not asking you to write a character study of Hibbert or to write down everything that he does and says in the play. You have to think about how the character 'works'. For example, you could consider how his fear represents an understandable reaction to life on the front or how Stanhope shows leadership by keeping Hibbert in the trenches.

EXAMINER'S TIPS

Remember to use **quotations** from the play as evidence to back up your ideas. The quotations do not have to be long but they do need to be **relevant**.

Source text 2.1

ARTHUR MILLER: *A View from the Bridge*

Catherine enters from bedroom; under his gaze she adjusts her dress.

CATHERINE: You got home early.

This is taken from the beginning section of Act 2.
Due to copyright restrictions, the full extract of
A View from the Bridge cannot be printed here;
however, you will have access to a full extract in
your exam.

RODOLPHO: *[with tears of rage]* Don't say that to me!

Rodolpho flies at him in attack. Eddie pins his arms, laughing, and suddenly kisses him.

Sample task 2.1

1a How does Miller make this such a dramatic moment in the play?   [40]

Student response 2.1

shows attention to wording of the question

Miller makes this scene from the play very dramatic. In it Eddie kisses both Catherine and Rodolpho on the lips. Catherine is Eddie's niece; he took Catherine in when her mother died and she became a daughter to them. The way Eddie kisses her shows his feelings for her are not what a father should feel for a daughter.

understands significance of the kiss

apt reference to the wider play

Beatrice has known for some time that Eddie's feelings are not the right ones. In Act 1, when Eddie tells Rodolpho 'I'm only her uncle', Beatrice says 'Well then be an uncle then.' Kissing Rodolpho on the lips is the way Eddie tries to show Catherine that Rodolpho 'ain't straight'.

good use of quotation to illustrate point

understands cause of behaviour

It is important to remember that when Eddie kisses Catherine and Rodolpho he is drunk. It is nearly Christmas and a case of whisky disappeared when a ship was being unloaded. The longshoremen took the bottles and Miller says in a stage direction that Eddie has three of them.

relevant reference to stage directions

When Catherine comes out of the bedroom, she has to adjust her dress. Just before this scene, Catherine and Rodolpho went into the bedroom together when there

EXAMINER'S TIPS

- ✔ Bear the wording of the question in mind when you read through the passage in the exam and underline or circle specific features that you would like to comment on in your answer.

- ✔ Try to group linked ideas together before you start writing. You could mark related points with a symbol or number them. This will help you to structure a coherent response.

was no one else in the house. It is interesting that she adjusts her dress under Eddie's gaze. This suggests that he is looking too hard at her, in a way that an uncle should not look at his niece. The stage directions show that when Eddie sees that Rodolpho has also been in the bedroom he is shocked. 'His arm jerks slightly in shock.' He understands that Rodolpho and Catherine have been up to something in the bedroom and takes the chance to throw Rodolpho out.

This is a powerful moment because Catherine 'instantly turns' and walks out because she is making a clear statement that she is choosing to be with Rodolpho. It is also powerful because Catherine loves Eddie. The stage directions say 'Her sobs and pity and love for him break her composure.' Miller makes Catherine's inner conflict, leading to her loss of 'composure', very powerful here. She has come to see Eddie as a father figure and has not understood or taken in the warnings Beatrice has given her. Beatrice has already seen that, as far as Eddie is concerned, no man will be good enough for Catherine: 'If it was a prince came here for you it would be no different'. She also knows that Eddie's unconscious feelings for Catherine are the reason that even a prince wouldn't be good enough, something neither Eddie nor Catherine knows. When Beatrice tells Eddie the truth, 'You want somethin' else, Eddie, and you can never have her!' both Eddie and Catherine's unawareness leads them both to react 'in horror'. Eddie's sudden kissing of Catherine 'on the mouth' here suggests that Eddie's subconscious

Margin annotations:

- again, apt reference to stage directions
- good inference
- understands character's actions
- acknowledges Catherine's conflicting feelings
- could develop this further
- perceptive point backed up with well-chosen quotation
- effective use of embedded quotations

Student response 2.I continued

feelings have risen to the surface, although he still cannot recognize them for what they are. This is also such a powerful moment because of the conflict between Eddie and Rodolpho. Eddie cannot bear the idea of losing Catherine and certainly not to a man like Rodopho who, in Eddie's view 'ain't right'. Here Rodolpho nods at Eddie 'testingly' and therefore provocatively. By kissing Rodolpho, Eddie accepts the challenge and believes he has shown that Rodolpho, the 'submarine', is not a real man. Triumphantly just after the kiss he says to Catherine 'You see?' However, far from proving his point, Eddie has ensured that Catherine will leave his house to be with Rodolpho.

This is more than just a dramatic moment in the play. The audience will see it as a turning point, a moment that drives Catherine to Rodolpho, and Eddie to the Immigration Bureau and to his death.

emphasizes Eddie's opinion of Rodolpho

understands how events link together

EXAMINER'S COMMENTS OCR
RECOGNISING ACHIEVEMENT

- The student responds enthusiastically and critically to this moment in the play.
- There is clear understanding of two of the central issues: Eddie's lack of knowledge of himself and Catherine's lack of understanding of him.
- A little more could be made of Eddie's reasons for kissing Rodolpho and what he is trying to prove.
- The answer would also benefit from greater focus on Rodolpho.
- Overall, this answer is filled with material that the candidate has selected well. It is a top-band response.

SAMPLE TASKS

FOUNDATION TIER

Sample task 2.2

J.B. PRIESTLEY: *An Inspector Calls*

1b What do you think makes Inspector Goole such a fascinating character?

Remember to support your ideas with details from the play. [27]

Student response 2.2

evidence of a personal response

I think Inspector Goole is a fascinating character. His name sounds like 'ghoul' and I think this implies that he's come from some sort of 'other world' to upset the Birlings.

some reference to wider themes of the play

He first comes into the play when Mr Birling, Gerald and Eric are drinking port after dinner in Act 1 as Gerald and Sheila Birling have got engaged. Mr Birling has been lecturing Gerald and Eric, telling them how men should look after themselves and not worry about other people. We hear 'the sharp ring of a front door bell' and the Inspector has arrived.

understands Priestley's structure and purpose

It's as if he knew somehow what Mr Birling was saying and has come to set him right.

He comes to ask questions about a girl called Eva Smith who has recently died because 'she'd swallowed a lot of strong disinfectant'. She had committed suicide. Mr Birling at first says that the name means nothing to him, but the Inspector tells him that Mr Birling once employed her at his works and shows him a photograph of Eva. He doesn't show it to Gerald and Eric,

too much story telling here

Student response 2.2 continued

inaccurate

but he will show it to them later. It seems like the Inspector is trying to find out why Eva Smith topped herself and putting the blame on Mr Birling. Eric, who is drunk, joins the Inspector in blaming Mr Birling, 'It's about time you learnt to face a few responsibilities'. I think this makes Inspector Goole a fascinating character because he causes this argument in the Birling family.

language too informal

some effort to link with question

The Inspector says that after being fired by Mr Birling Eva got a job at a shop in Brumley called Milwards where Sheila does her clothes shopping. Sheila says she has never heard of Eva.

When the Inspector shows her the photograph she recognizes her. She was the assistant that Sheila had fired from Milwards. So she was partly to blame, 'But you're partly to blame. Just as your father is.'

understands writer's method here

not the best wording

By the end of the play we find out that all the members of the Birling family and Gerald had something to do with Eva Smith's suicide. Gerald found her in a bar and kept her as his mistress, two-timing Sheila while he was at it. Mrs Birling refused to help her when she asked and she'd gone to ask for money because Eric had got her pregnant. I think the Inspector is fascinating because he shows that they all had something to do with her swallowing 'a strong disinfectant'.

important quotation but this should be expanded upon

He is fascinating because he shows the family up and tries to teach them an important lesson, 'We are responsible for each other'.

EXAMINER'S COMMENTS OCR

- The student shows some knowledge of the overall plot.
- There are some references to the text and some use of quotation but this response does not select widely enough. It depends too much on Act 1 and Mr Birling's and Sheila's behaviour.
- Gerald, Mrs Birling and Eric are given little attention. A clear plan might have helped the student to cover more material in the time given.
- There is some attempt to focus on the question, but this is inconsistent.
- This is a lower-band response.

Unit 3

Prose From Different Cultures

HOW TO APPROACH UNIT 3

What will be assessed in this unit?

Unit 3 focuses on the study of prose texts from a variety of cultures. You will study one of the following texts:

- *Of Mice and Men* by John Steinbeck
- *To Kill a Mockingbird* by Harper Lee
- *Anita and Me* by Meera Syal
- *Paddy Clarke Ha Ha Ha* by Roddy Doyle
- *Tsotsi* by Athol Fugard
- *The Joy Luck Club* by Amy Tan.

Although you may not have direct experience of being a migrant worker in California, of being a victim of racial abuse in Alabama or of struggling to survive in a South African township, you may still be familiar with the problems and dilemmas faced by the characters in these novels. Discrimination, prejudice and conflicts between different cultures and generations are all issues that many people will face at some time in their lives.

How will I be assessed?

This unit will be tested in an exam lasting **45 minutes**. There will be two questions set on each text, and you will select **one** question to answer. This unit is worth 25% of your English Literature GCSE.

You will be tested on the Assessment Objectives listed below:

- **AO2: Explain how language, structure and form contribute to writers' presentation of ideas, themes and settings.**
  This means that you need to show an overall understanding of the language features, structure and form that the writer has used and be able to explain the effects these produce on the reader.

- **AO4: Relate texts to their social, cultural and historical contexts; explain how texts have been influential and significant to self and other readers in different contexts and at different times.** Your main task is to discuss, criticize and analyse the text. Your knowledge of the social, cultural and historical context should be sufficient for you to understand your text; it should not require you to do hours of background research.

How can I find out about the contexts of my set text?

Reading your set text should give you enough knowledge about the key contextual issues to equip you for your exam preparation. You might need to check small background details but there is no need to embark on an in-depth study of the period in which the novel was set or learn endless facts about the politics of the time. For example, in *To Kill a Mockingbird* Harper Lee makes clear how the characters are affected by issues such as prejudice, poverty and views of 'justice'.

An intelligent read of the text and willingness to look up key facts to support your knowledge should be sufficient to allow you to understand the context of the novel.

As with some of the texts in the other units, you might find a film version helps your understanding of the setting, plot and characters. However, remember that the content of the **text** is what you will be examined on, not what is in the film. Note that the two are not always the same!

Passage-Based Questions

LEARNING CHECKLIST

In this chapter you will learn to:

1 Explain how the writer uses language, structure and form to present ideas, themes and settings.

2 Link texts to their social, cultural and historical backgrounds; explain the influence of texts on yourself and different readers in different places and times.

Choosing a passage-based question

If you choose to answer the passage-based question in the Unit 3 exam, you will need to look very closely at the extract from your chosen text. Usually, you will be asked to explore how the writer portrays a character or presents a theme, or how a specific moment in the action is made interesting or powerful for the reader. You will also need to consider how the writer uses language and form to convey ideas.

You will need to show an appreciation of when the text was written and where it is set. Attitudes and values change over time and differ depending on the culture. This can influence both the writer and different readers of a text. For example, a reader reading about Victorian England might interpret the book differently to someone living in 19th-century America. You must be able to show you understand this idea in your answer. Below is one way of approaching a passage-based question.

1 Read the question twice and underline key words.

2 Then read the extract at least twice, highlighting and underlining words and phrases you think are relevant to your question. Consider:

- which parts are most useful and which quotations you can use
- how another sense of time and place is created through the writer's use of language
- how the characters' attitudes are different from those of today
- how this extract relates to other parts of the novel
- who is telling the story and how they tell it.

You need to read the passage through twice and underline <u>key words</u>

The question below is similar to one you might face in the exam. It would be printed after a specific extract from the set text. Notice how a student has annotated the question to check exactly what is being asked.

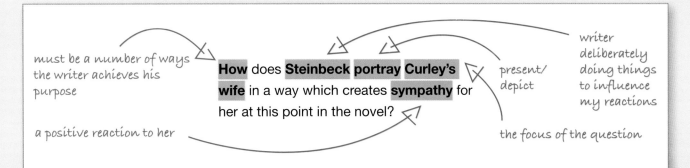

must be a number of ways the writer achieves his purpose

a positive reaction to her

How does **Steinbeck** **portray** **Curley's** **wife** in a way which creates **sympathy** for her at this point in the novel?

present/ depict

writer deliberately doing things to influence my reactions

the focus of the question

ACTIVITY I

Add your own annotations to copies of the questions given below. Identify what the examiner is asking you to do in relation to the passage. You do not need to be familiar with the novels or particular extracts in order to analyse what the questions are asking.

This question is about Meera Syal's novel *Anita and Me*:

> ii) How does Syal's writing here vividly reveal that Anita and Meena come from different worlds?

This question is about Roddy Doyle's book, *Paddy Clarke Ha Ha Ha*:

> i) Explore the ways in which Doyle portrays the relationship between Paddy's parents at this moment in the novel.

EXAMINER'S TIPS

✔ When preparing for this exam, remember that it is important to have an understanding of the whole text. Even if you choose to answer a passage-based question in the exam, knowledge of the full plot, characters and setting is essential if you are to analyse the passage effectively.

✔ If you choose to answer a passage-based question, your response should focus primarily on the passage, but you should think about the significance of the passage in the novel as a whole.

Showing awareness of differences

When writing about a text from a different culture or time, you need to show that you understand how the attitudes of the characters in the text are different to those of today. Things that were considered acceptable in the past may not be acceptable at all today. In addition, what is deemed acceptable in one country, or culture, may be offensive in another.

Read the statements below taken from *Of Mice and Men*, a novel set in America during the 1930s.

UNIT 3

'I tell ya, you got floozy idears about what us guys amounts to. You ain't got sense enough in that chicken head. to even see that we ain't stiffs.'

'I wisht somebody'd shoot me if I got old an' a cripple.'

'They play cards in there, but I can't play because I'm black. They say I stink.'

'Whyn't you get Candy to shoot his old dog… Candy feeds him milk. He can't chew nothing else.'

ACTIVITY 2

Identify the prejudice in each of the statements above and explain how our attitudes today are different.

Language choices and quotations

When you are writing about a text, the points that you make need to be supported by quotations and then discussed. You need to show awareness of how the writer uses language to create particular effects on the reader; for example, his or her choice of vocabulary, phrases and imagery.

Read the extract below from *To Kill a Mockingbird*.

From *To Kill a Mockingbird* by Harper Lee

Maycomb was an old town, but it was a tired old town when I first knew it. In rainy weather the streets turned to red slop; grass grew on the sidewalks, the courthouse sagged in the square. Somehow, it was hotter then: a black dog suffered on a summer's day; bony mules hitched to Hoover carts flicked flies in the sweltering shade of the live oaks on the square. Men's stiff collars wilted by nine in the morning. Ladies bathed before noon, after their three o' clock naps, and by nightfall were like soft teacakes with frostings of sweat and sweet talcum.

ACTIVITY 3

Complete the grid below to explore how the author uses language features to create an impression of Maycomb as a town in decline.

QUOTATION	LANGUAGE FEATURE	ANALYSIS/ COMMENT
'a tired old town'		suggests a dilapidated place in need of rejuvenation and development
	alliteration	reinforces sense that the heat is unavoidable and stifling
'Men's stiff collars wilted'	metaphor	
	simile	implies the heat counteracts the women's attempts to look fashionable

ACTIVITY 4

Write a paragraph about how the author successfully portrays Maycomb as a southern American town in decline during the Great Depression of the 1930s. Use the grid to the right and the quotations below to help you.

'a day was twenty-four hours long but seemed longer'

'there was nowhere to go'

'His first two clients were the last two persons hanged in the Maycomb County jail.'

'They did not go to church, Maycomb's principal recreation.'

Different social and cultural settings

Society's attitude towards many things varies according to time and place. For example, attitudes towards women in the 1930s were different from those commonly held today.

Here are some quotations from *Of Mice and Men* (set in the USA in the 1930s). They are all linked to Curley's wife. Some are made by the men working on the ranch; others are spoken by Curley's wife.

'a tart'

'she's purty'

'she's a rat trap'

'bet she'd clear out for twenty bucks'

'she got the eye'

'he's keepin that hand soft for his wife'

'I get lonely'

'You got no call foolin' aroun' with other guys, causin' trouble'

'good lookin'

'...I can't talk to nobody but Curley. Else he gets mad.'

'I seen her give Slim the eye'

'...the discontent and the ache for attention were all gone from her face'

'what a tramp'

'Ain't I got a right to talk to nobody'

'bitch'

'her face was sweet and young'

'I don't like Curley. He ain't a nice fella'.

ACTIVITY 5

Read the quotations above and decide which create sympathy for Curley's wife and which create dislike for her.

When answering a passage-based question, you will need to focus primarily on the printed extract, but you also need to expand your answer to show wider knowledge and understanding of the whole novel.

The text below is from a student's essay about Curley's wife and the social and cultural attitudes towards women at the time. Here, the student is widening her subject beyond the printed passage to demonstrate her knowledge of the novel and the context in which it was written.

STUDENT

The men on the ranch treat Curley's wife shamefully. Even her husband talks about her in a way that is disrespectful and ___. As the only woman on the ranch she is an ___ and ___ figure. Her flirtatious nature is ___ by the men as sexual ___. However, the author is actually presenting a young woman who is ___ in a loveless and damaging marriage. Her flirtatious nature is better interpreted as a desperate attempt to make contact with others. Steinbeck uses Curley's wife to reveal the ___ attitudes towards women that ___ in America during the 1930s when the novel was written. He presents a ___ society that sees women as merely sexual objects and which ___ them. Although sexism exists today, there is a much greater sense of equality between men and women.

ACTIVITY 6

Read the extract from the student's essay carefully, inserting the missing words below in the appropriate gaps. Use a dictionary to look up any words that you are unsure of.

immorality

belittling

isolated   existed   sexist

alienated   interpreted

negative   trapped   degrades

EXAMINER'S TIPS

Do not try to write a complete essay on the context of the prose text you are studying. Stick closely to answering the question that you are being asked, and that will automatically give you an opportunity to show your knowledge of the context of the text.

Different political and historical settings

Novels that are set in the past reflect the history of that period. Writers will often show the different social and political viewpoints of the time through the characters that they create.

Read the extract below from Athol Fugard's novel *Tsotsi*, which is set in a South African township during apartheid. The extract describes the main character, a violent gang leader. Although this description is about one young man, Tsotsi is representative of thousands of black men in South Africa, who responded with violence to the repressive, racist white government.

From *Tsotsi*
by Athol Fugard

Tsotsi hated the questions for a profound but simple reason. He didn't know the answers… neither his name, nor his age, nor any of the other answers that men assemble and shape into the semblance of a life. His memory went back vaguely to a group of young boys scavenging the township for scraps needed to keep alive. Before that a few vague, moody memories, a police chase and finding himself alone. Tsotsi didn't know because he had never been told, and if he had once known he no longer remembered, and his not knowing himself had a deeper meaning than his name and his age. His own eyes in front of a mirror had not been able to put together the eyes, and the nose, and the mouth and the chin, and make a man with a meaning. His own features in his own eyes had been meaningless as a handful of stones picked up at random in the street outside his room. He allowed himself no thought of himself, he remembered no yesterdays, and tomorrow existed only when it was the present, living moment. He was as old as that moment, and his name was the name, in a way, of all men.

ACTIVITY 7

a Find quotations from the extract to back up the points below that Fugard makes about life for black people living under apartheid:

- their sense of identity had been taken apart
- they felt devalued and dehumanized
- they lived lives without hope
- poverty surrounded them
- they were left searching for answers they couldn't find
- surviving was all that mattered
- individuals felt isolated
- remembering the past was a difficult experience.

b What do you think the author means by saying 'his not knowing himself had a deeper meaning than his name and age'? Think about all the things that make up a person's identity and how much of this Tsotsi lacks.

EXTENSION TASK

How might the character Tsotsi be seen as a metaphor for the whole country of South Africa? Write a short paragraph to explore this idea.

Consider:

- a country unsure of its own identity
- a country with a complicated and difficult past
- a country full of pain and suffering.

ACTIVITY 8

The author uses two similes in this extract:

- his features were 'meaningless as a handful of stones picked up at random in the street'
- 'He was as old as that moment'.

Explain what effects the writer creates with these comparisons.

STOP APARTHEID NOW!

Comment, Criticism and Analysis

LEARNING CHECKLIST

In this chapter you will learn to:

1 Explain how the writer uses language, structure and form to present ideas, themes and settings.

2 Link texts to their social, cultural and historical backgrounds; explain the influence of texts on yourself and different readers in different places and times.

Commenting on texts

The focus of this chapter is on how to respond to questions that require comment, criticism and analysis. For example, you may be asked to **comment** on how the author shows the development of a character or a theme. You may need to **critically** evaluate how effectively an author creates a sympathetic character or an exciting conflict. You may need to **analyse** how particular episodes are made more significant by the structure or language used.

Understanding context

The novel you have been studying was chosen not only because of its literary worth, but also because it requires understanding of a different culture and perhaps a different historical period. You should explore its setting, the characters' beliefs and the expectations of their communities. The characters – from a Catholic boy in Dublin to labourers in California – do not exist in isolation; they are affected by the concerns, priorities and events that surround them.

ACTIVITY I

Look at the list of contextual factors below and make a note of any that apply to the novel you are studying:

- set in a country outside the United Kingdom
- set in the United Kingdom, but features characters from a different country
- set more than 50 years ago
- deals with political issues
- deals with social issues
- explores the religious beliefs of the characters
- explores areas of conflict between communities.

Narrative voice

Every novel has a narrator: someone who tells the story. However, there are different types of **narrative voice**. Some narrators are hardly noticeable while others are distinctive. The two main types of narrative voice are described below.

FIRST-PERSON NARRATOR	THIRD-PERSON NARRATOR
Told by a character in the novel. Uses 'I/we'. May have gaps in knowledge. Writing may be conversational and informal. Note that there may be multiple first-person narrators in a novel.	Written in the third person: uses 'he/she/they'. May be omniscient (all-knowing). Usually more objectively and formally written.

ACTIVITY 2

Read the extracts in the panels. With a partner, discuss what type of narrator each one has.

> This was terrible; in front of the others, I couldn't sort out my little brother.

> Tsotsi feared nothingness. He feared it because he believed in it.

> My stomach turned to water and I nearly threw up when Jem held out the blanket and crept toward me.

> I do not have many memories of my very early childhood, apart from the obvious ones, of course.

> George's voice became deeper. He repeated his words rhythmically as though he had said them many times before.

Another type of narrator is an **unreliable narrator**, whose perceptions are not necessarily to be trusted. Here is an extract from *Anita and Me*.

> I'm really not a liar, I just learned very early on that those of us deprived of history sometimes need to turn to mythology to feel complete, to belong.

ACTIVITY 3

In the extract to the left, what reason does the narrator give for lying? Do you trust this narrator?

EXTENSION TASK

Using the extract as inspiration, write your own opening to a novel. Try to create a distinctive narrative voice.

Characterization

A good novel will enable you to bring the characters to life in your mind. Perhaps you can imagine what they look like, how they sound and even what they are thinking. When analysing characters, you should consider how they are described, their dialogue, how they interact with other characters and their importance to the plot.

Often the main character in a novel will go on an emotional or psychological 'journey'. He or she may begin the novel in a state of innocence or ignorance and then, through a series of events, gain experience and knowledge. Look at the flow diagram below which highlights Paddy Clarke's development in *Paddy Clarke Ha Ha Ha*.

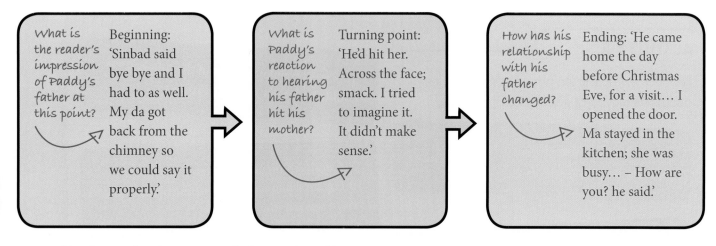

What is the reader's impression of Paddy's father at this point?

Beginning: 'Sinbad said bye bye and I had to as well. My da got back from the chimney so we could say it properly.'

What is Paddy's reaction to hearing his father hit his mother?

Turning point: 'He'd hit her. Across the face; smack. I tried to imagine it. It didn't make sense.'

How has his relationship with his father changed?

Ending: 'He came home the day before Christmas Eve, for a visit… I opened the door. Ma stayed in the kitchen; she was busy… – How are you? he said.'

Read a student's response below and see if you agree with her analysis of Paddy Clarke's development as a character.

STUDENT

Early in the novel, Paddy's father is shown entertaining his children at Christmas, which makes him seem kind. However, there are hints of tension in the family, which young Paddy cannot fully understand. When he hears the 'smack', his relationship with his father changes. At the end, the two are almost strangers to each other, speaking formally and politely, but without the previous warmth. Paddy has learned about the adult world and is no longer the same carefree boy.

EXAMINER'S TIPS

When writing about characters in this unit, you should avoid creating general character studies. The questions will often prompt you to think about how writers **use** characters to convey important **ideas** in their novels.

Setting and culture

Where a novel is set is important to our understanding of the characters and their behaviour. Characters are products of their environment. They have absorbed the traditions, priorities and values of the country in which they were raised. Sometimes they remain in the countries in which they were born and sometimes they leave them.

In *Anita and Me*, Meena's parents have moved from India to the English village of Tollington but they retain a love for their 'ancestral home' in India.

Read the extract below, which describes Meena's parents' first married home in New Delhi, and consider the questions that annotate it.

How is this different from a typical British home?

What sort of weather might you associate with this home? What colours feature in this extract?

From *Anita and Me*
by Meera Syal

Mama had just begun her first teaching job and they lived in a whitewashed single-storey flat-roofed house. I knew this from one of the photos, where they are sitting on a bed in a courtyard, a low bed strung across with hessian mesh which bends under their weight. Just visible on the stone courtyard floor is a dull stain the size of an orange, which papa told me happened when he squashed a passing scorpion under his *chappal*. Papa sits behind mama, has his arms around her just like Sam Lowbridge with his 'wenches' in the park. They are both in white cotton which catches the sunlight and emphasises the nutty brown of their skin. They are laughing, they are at that moment exactly where they want to be.

Is this comparison surprising?

How is it suggested that her parents are happy in this environment?

ACTIVITY 4

Find an extract from *Anita and Me* that shows how Meena's parents react to their environment in Tollington. Write a paragraph contrasting their environments in England and India.

ACTIVITY 5

Choose a passage from the novel you are studying that describes an important location.

a What techniques does the author use to make it vivid?

b Discuss with a partner how the location affects the characters in the novel.

Exploring themes

A theme is a significant idea that an author explores in his or her work; sometimes there will be a number of themes in a novel. Many of the novels chosen for this unit share themes with other works from the 20th and 21st centuries. For example, commonly occuring themes are loneliness, isolation and uncertainty about personal identity.

ACTIVITY 6

Look at the list of themes below and note down any which you think apply to the novel you are studying:

- loneliness
- identity
- childhood
- injustice
- friendship
- education
- prejudice.

Several of the novels being studied are written from a child's point of view and provide insight into the young lives of the characters. The spider diagram below shows how you might explore the theme of childhood.

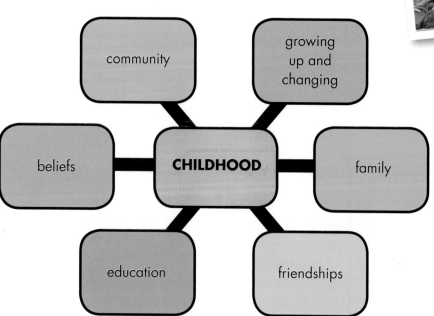

```
        community          growing
                           up and
                           changing

  beliefs      CHILDHOOD           family

        education          friendships
```

ACTIVITY 7

Create your own spider diagram, exploring either childhood or another theme in the novel you are studying. Find quotations from the novel to support your ideas.

Prejudice, injustice and racism

The last century was one of great political and social change and the novels written during this century reflect the shifting attitudes of society. Novelists often focus on the plight of characters who are treated unfairly due to the colour of their skin, their religious affiliations or simply because they are 'different'. Sometimes a novelist is seeking to influence readers, making them aware of injustices from the past or of prejudices that still exist today.

When investigating this theme it is essential that you look at the social attitudes at the time in which the book is set. For example, China before the Second World War – the world of the mothers in *The Joy Luck Club* – is very different from San Francisco in the 1980s, which influences their daughters. In *To Kill a Mockingbird*, Atticus Finch's bravery in representing Tom Robinson is unusual in the American South of the 1930s. In *Tsotsi*, the protagonist represents the plight of millions of black people who suffered under the apartheid regime in South Africa.

ACTIVITY 8

Considering the theme of prejudice, respond to the following bullet points in relation to the novel you are studying.

- Describe any characters who are treated unfairly because they are perceived as being 'different' or inferior in some way.
- List at least three instances from the novel in which a character suffers from prejudicial treatment.
- How does the character react to this unfair treatment? Provide quotations.
- At the end of the novel, who suffers due to the prejudice?
- What point do you think the author is making about prejudice?

Language, structure and form

When writing about your chosen novel, you need to show that you understand how the author uses language, structure and form to convey his or her ideas. In literature, you must search for the use of subtle techniques to create a mood or explore an idea. There is often a meaning beyond the words on the page. Look carefully for the order in which the writer presents his or her ideas, the repetition of certain images or the connections between events and ideas.

Techniques that authors use include metaphor, simile, alliteration, symbolism and personification. What techniques do you notice in the extract below from *To Kill a Mockingbird*?

What impression do we get of the Radley Place?

What technique is used here and what is its effect?

What technique is used and what does it tell us about the house's appearance?

What mood does Harper Lee create in this passage?

From *To Kill a Mockingbird*
by Harper Lee

The Radley Place jutted into a sharp curve beyond our house. Walking south, one faced its porch; the sidewalk turned and ran beside the lot. The house was low, was once white with a deep front porch and green shutters, but had long ago darkened to the colour of the slate-grey yard around it. Rain-rotten shingles drooped over the eaves of the veranda; oak trees kept the sun away. The remains of a picket drunkenly guarded the front yard – a 'swept' yard that was never swept – where johnson grass and rabbit-tobacco grew in abundance.

Inside the house lived a malevolent phantom.

ACTIVITY 9

Choose a passage from your novel which uses language in an interesting way. Highlight any examples of devices the writer uses to create a strong impression or atmosphere.

EXTENSION TASK

Carefully note the writing style of your chosen author and write a new paragraph in his or her style. Remember to consider vocabulary, sentence structure and tone.

Bringing together your ideas

Remembering to **comment**, **criticize** and **analyse**, complete the following tasks showing that you can express your understanding of language, form and structure, as well as the context of the novel. Remember that you must use specific evidence from the text and comment on how the author achieves his or her effects.

ACTIVITY 10

Choose one of the main characters in the novel you are studying and explain how his or her feelings and thoughts are expressed at the end of the novel.

To prepare to answer this question, copy and complete the following grid:

CHARACTER'S NAME	POINT	EVIDENCE FROM TEXT
What are the character's feelings and thoughts at the end of the novel?		
How have the character's feelings and thoughts changed?		
How does the author use language to show what the character is feeling and thinking?		
How does the context of the novel influence what the character is feeling and thinking?		

ACTIVITY 11

Read the extract to the right, which is taken from a student's response. How would you extend or improve this student's paragraph about Miriam in *Tsotsi*?

STUDENT

At the end of the novel, Miriam has accepted that her husband will never come home, yet she is determined to 'manage'. The 'brave' whiteness of her washing symbolizes hope for her and her son's future. She has rejected the bitterness she previously felt, comparing it to her milk going sour, and instead realizes that she has enough love and compassion to offer even a stranger.

TRY THIS!

Drama and media explorations

Curley's wife is an important character in *Of Mice and Men* and John Steinbeck provides a number of clues about her life and dreams. Use the activities below to develop your understanding of her role in the novel and some of the challenges facing women at that time.

ACTIVITY 1

In pairs, role-play the meeting between Curley's wife and the man who said he was in the film business and could make her a star. What do we learn about both of these characters from this encounter?

ACTIVITY 2

a In pairs, improvise the encounter between Curley's wife and her mother when she says she wants to go to Hollywood.

b Discuss who you think is right – Curley's wife or her mother? Consider:
   • what options for escape there are for Curley's wife
   • what jobs or opportunities exist for her
   • what the typical role of women was in the 1930s.

c Write an alternative version of this scene which leads to a happier ending for Curley's wife.

ACTIVITY 3

Research the films of the 1930s which may have appealed to Curley's wife. Collect images of stars, costumes and themes from this time and decide which star she would most like to resemble. Design a poster showing the sort of film in which she could imagine starring.

ACTIVITY 4

a Choose an important incident from the novel you are studying and 'hot-seat' the characters to establish their feelings towards the event. For example, hot-seat the main characters in *To Kill a Mockingbird* after Tom Robinson's trial; any witnesses to the fight between Kevin and Paddy in *Paddy Clarke Ha Ha Ha* or Tsotsi's acquaintances after he beats up Boston in *Tsotsi*.

b Choose one of the characters and prepare a short statement about how he or she feels. In the role of that character, answer questions from the other students about the event. Consider:

- what you know about the event
- what happened afterwards
- if you feel any regret, responsibility or guilt.

ACTIVITY 5

Write an article for a local newspaper reporting on a significant event from the novel you are studying, such as the death of Curley's wife, the trial of Tom Robinson or the accident at Morris Tshabalala's mineshaft. If possible, research newspapers from the time and place in which the novel is set in order to capture the tone as accurately as possible. Write using the correct form for a newspaper article, including a headline and interviews with witnesses.

EXTENSION TASK

Choose a supporting character from your novel and write a diary extract imagining what that character's life is like and what his or her perspective is on the main characters and events in the novel. For example, you might choose a character such as Charles Leavy (*Paddy Clarke Ha Ha Ha*); Candy or Crooks (*Of Mice and Men*); Mrs Dubose or Calpurnia (*To Kill a Mockingbird*); Boston or Miriam Ngidi (*Tsotsi*) or Uncle Alan or Fat Sally (*Anita and Me*).

PREPARING FOR UNIT 3

What will the questions be like?

In the exam you will have to answer **one** question from a choice of two, on the novel you have studied. One question will be passage-based, and one will be more general, asking you to comment, criticize and analyse.

When responding to the **passage-based question**, most of your answer needs to be focused on the actual extract provided on the exam paper. However, it is also good to show a wider knowledge of the novel and an understanding of why the passage provided is significant. The extract will have been chosen because it is important; either in terms of the plot or the setting, or because it raises particular themes that are key to the play as a whole. It may also have been selected because it reveals something interesting about character development.

The more **general question** will expect you to refer to the novel more widely rather than concentrating on one particular extract. It could relate to a specific episode or it might trace a particular theme or character throughout the whole novel.

How long should I spend on my answer?

You have **45 minutes** to answer your chosen question. Do spend some of this time choosing which question to answer and planning your response.

How will my work be marked?

If you are entered at **Foundation tier**, your answer will be marked out of **27**. Some of the questions may include prompts in the form of bullet points, which provide guidance on what aspects you should consider in your answer. If you are entered at **Higher tier**, your answer will be marked out of **40**.

EXAMINER'S TIPS

Whichever question you choose to answer, remember to refer closely to the text, using **quotations** and details to back up the points that you are making. Single word quotations are often as effective as whole phrases or sentences.

How can I prepare for this exam?

Everyone prepares for exams in different ways but here are some suggestions that you may find useful:

Make sure you know the text well.

When you've read it carefully, two, three or four times, read sections of it again for perhaps 15 minutes at a time to keep the text fresh in your memory.

Find out what sample or past papers look like.

Your exam board, OCR, has prepared sample question papers that your teacher will be able to supply you with; they can also be found on OCR's website (www.ocr.org.uk).

Look carefully at the type of questions examiners are asking.

While you will be expected to demonstrate your knowledge of the social, cultural or historical contexts of the text you are studying, the question is unlikely to ask you about this directly. For example, there won't be a question on *To Kill a Mockingbird* like 'What do you learn about the life of black people in *To Kill a Mockingbird*?' You may, however, be asked a question such as 'What do you find so shocking about the trial of Tom Robinson?' This will be testing your knowledge of the novel and its cultural background.

Remember that you must answer the question.

Don't feel that you must write down all you know about the background of the novel to satisfy AO4. If you focus on the question you have been asked, what you know will be clear from your answer.

HIGHER TIER

Sample task 3.1

1b How does Harper Lee make the Ewell family so memorable and significant in *To Kill a Mockingbird*?

Remember to support your ideas with details from the novel. [40]

Student response 3.1

The Ewells are a large family. Bob Ewell is the father, but the mother is dead and has been for a long time.

some background but no indication of why the family is significant

The author, Harper Lee, describes three members of the family, Mayella, Bob Ewell and Burris Ewell.

On Scout's first day at school, she is soon in trouble with her teacher, Miss Caroline Fisher, because she explains that Walter Cunningham comes from a family that never takes anything they can't pay back. Miss Fisher has tried to lend Walter a

good reference back to the question

quarter for his lunch. Harper Lee uses Scout's first day at school to introduce characters who will be important later in the novel.

no mention of the Ewells, but good point about introducing characters

Burris Ewell is used to introduce us to the Ewell family. Burris is a memorable character. Scout says 'He was the filthiest human I had ever seen. His neck was dark grey, the backs of his hands were rusty, and his finger-nails were black deep into the quick'. He is also memorable because a 'cootie' has crawled out of his hair, scaring Miss Caroline Fisher. Burris can't spell his name, as he is illiterate, and only comes to school on the first

well selected quotation

Student response 3.1 continued

another apt quotation

day of the year and is marked absent for the rest of the year. He is a bully and a coward. He makes Miss Caroline cry as he leaves the classroom shouting 'Ain't no snot-nosed slut of a schoolteacher ever born c'n make me do nothin'.' Then the text says, 'He waited until he was sure she was crying, then he shuffled out of the building', showing that he is a bully.

good link between son and father

shows knowledge of the narrative

He is also scared of Little Chuck Little who is described as being 'half his height' showing that he is a coward. Burris is memorable because he prepares us for his father, Bob Ewell, who we see is also a bully and a coward. He hits his daughter and at the end of the novel he tries to kill two children, Jem and Scout, to get back at Atticus for making him look a fool in the court.

awareness of the culture and society

The Ewells appear in the courtroom scene. Tom Robinson, a black man, is accused of raping Mayella. Jem and Scout find out that the Ewells live behind 'the town garbage dump in what was once a Negro cabin'. This means that, although they are white, they are below even the black community in the social scale.

the student's choice of language could be better here

too much focus on storytelling rather than the question

The trial scene is the most memorable part of the whole novel. Basically, Mayella who is very lonely, fancies Tom Robinson. She asks him in one day to chop up a 'chiffarobe' and grabs him round the legs. Tom Robinson was a victim of Mayella who fancied him and Bob Ewell who accused him of raping Mayella.

cultural awareness

Despite all the evidence the jury find Tom Robinson guilty. He is later shot trying to escape from the jail.

Atticus really shows everyone, even in the racially prejudiced town, that Tom Robinson is innocent.

EXAMINER'S TIPS

Remember, in the exam you will have the choice of either answering the passage-based question (part **a**) **or** the question requiring comment, criticism and analysis (part **b**).

Student response 3.1 continued

He is a mockingbird that does not harm and it is a sin that he is killed.

good observation

Bob Ewell wants revenge because Atticus has made a fool of him in court. As he is about to kill Jem and Scout, Boo Radley, who has always watched over them, comes and saves them. So the Ewells are significant as if it wasn't for them Scout would not have met Boo Radley at the end of the novel.

The Ewell family is very significant in the novel. If it wasn't for them, Tom Robinson would never have died.

conclusion effectively addresses the question

EXAMINER'S COMMENTS OCR

- The structure of the response is weak. There is too much focus on the school section and too little analysis of the way the Ewells behave at the trial and the injustice suffered by Tom Robinson.

- The conclusion seems hurried and just summarizes events, although the student sensibly keeps the wording of the question in mind.

- There is over-dependence on re-telling the story, rather than answering the question.

- A lower-band response.

FOUNDATION TIER

Source text 3.2

ATHOL FUGARD: *Tsotsi*

It was a young woman, a black woman, coming towards him in the night. She was wearing a long coat, unbuttoned, and underneath it he could see a white garment that could have been a petticoat. She carried a small parcel and she kept on looking back.

From his position under the tree Tsotsi recognized without hesitation   5
the symptoms of fear. Nothing else moved a human being the same way. He had seen it often. She held her parcel as if it were her last hold on life itself. Even if their hands were empty, they would hold themselves, hand holding hand. She was nearer now and he could see that her parcel was a shoebox. Fear too, and fear alone, made you see a threat of danger in   10
every shadow, which is how she was, her head turning constantly from side to side. But most of all fear made you hurry. She was caught in an ungainly rhythm between walking and running, almost tripping over her feet in her hurry. Once or twice, with a few steps quicker than the rest, it seemed she was about to break into a run, but each time something stopped her and   15
she fell back into her stumbling lope.

Tsotsi watched her from under the trees. Without realizing it, his heart began to beat faster. It was almost perfect. The woman came towards him in the night, he didn't know her, he didn't hate, but he slipped slyly from tree to tree to the point where she would enter the grove. He didn't know what   20
he was going to do but his fingers flexed at his side. His hands were ready.

She was opposite him now, having paused on her way to lean against a wall and shake her head. She crossed the street and walked into the grove of bluegum trees.

He caught her by one arm and swung her into the darkness, his   25
hand cutting short the scream of terror that had fallen from her lips like splintering glass.

A second move forced her against a tree and there, with his body pressed against hers, a knee already between her legs and his hand still on her mouth, there he looked into her eyes. She struggled once but he held   30
her firmly. She clutched her shoebox with even greater desperation.

Sample task 3.2

1a What do you think is so disturbing and interesting about this extract?

You should consider:

- the woman's fear
- Tsotsi
- the shoebox
- the words and phrases Fugard uses. [27]

Student response 3.2

The way Athol Fugard describes the woman is very disturbing and interesting. She is afraid of something as she keeps looking back as if someone is chasing her, but we don't know what she is afraid of. She is in a hurry and hasn't dressed properly as it says her coat is unbuttoned and if the white is the white of a petticoat she is not wearing a dress or a skirt. She is very afraid as it says 'Fear too, and fear alone, made you see a threat of danger in every shadow, which is how she was, her head turning constantly from side to side. But most of all fear made you hurry.' She is hurrying so much that she was 'almost tripping over her feet in her hurry'.

    It is disturbing that she doesn't know that Tsosti is in 'the grove of bluegum trees' watching her. Tsotsi loves hurting and killing people. He has just killed Gumboot Dhlamini and beaten Boston up. The woman is running away from something and doesn't know that she is running into danger.

immediate focus on the question

could draw out more of a sense of mystery

good focus on the text but a closer analysis of this would gain more marks

shows knowledge of the wider text

links back to question

EXAMINER'S TIPS

Looking at and discussing the **language** writers use to create particular effects will help you to gain higher marks.

Student response 3.2 continued

valid idea but needs to link to 'disturbing' →

I think Tsotsi is going to rape her: 'His heart began to beat faster. It was almost perfect. The woman came towards him in the night, he didn't know her, he didn't hate, but he slyly slipped from tree to tree to the point where she would enter the grove.' Then he presses his body against hers, 'a knee already between her legs'.

The shoebox is mentioned several times and it matters a lot to the woman. 'She clutched her shoebox with even greater desperation.' After this she shoves the shoebox at Tsotsi and runs away. When Tsotsi opens the shoebox he finds a baby in it. I think it is interesting that the shoebox is so important to the woman and then she gives it to a complete stranger.

valid personal response and relevant link back to the question

EXAMINER'S COMMENTS OCR

- There is a lot of quotation here, but this student needs to comment more on the words and phrases; for example, 'slyly slipped', the woman's 'desperation' and her scream 'like splintering glass'. How do these language choices impact the reader?

- The student discusses what happens in the passage but does not reflect on how the writer has chosen to sequence it. The student could have considered how the order of events works to build suspense, which makes the passage more disturbing and more interesting.

- A fuller answer would explore the passage in more detail and make tighter, more consistent links to the question.

- This response is somewhere in the lower band. Closer comments on the language used in the passage would push it up to the next band.

Unit 4

Literary Heritage Prose and Contemporary Poetry

HOW TO APPROACH UNIT 4

How will I be assessed?

This unit is tested by an exam in which you will answer **two** questions:

- one question on a Literary Heritage Prose text
- one question on **either** a selection of poems by one contemporary poet **or** unseen poetry.

The exam lasts for an hour and a half, so you should spend **45 minutes** on **each question**. This unit is worth 25% of your English Literature GCSE.

What will I be assessed on?

In the Unit 4 exam, you will be tested on the Assessment Objectives listed below.

AO1: Respond to texts critically and imaginatively; select and evaluate relevant textual detail to illustrate and support interpretations.

This means that you need to show how you understand and interpret the text, using quotations to explain your ideas and responses.

AO2: Explain how language, structure and form contribute to writers' presentation of ideas, themes and settings.

This means that you need to show an overall understanding of the language features, structure and form that the writer has used and be able to explain the effects these produce on the reader.

As in all the units for English Literature, the quality of your 'written communication' will be assessed. This means that you need to:

- ensure your text is legible, and that spelling, punctuation and grammar are accurate so that meaning is clear
- present information in a form that suits its purpose
- use a suitable structure and style of writing.

What is the choice of texts to study?

In this section you will study **one** of the following texts:

- *Pride and Prejudice* by Jane Austen
- *Silas Marner* by George Eliot
- *Lord of the Flies* by William Golding
- *The Withered Arm and other Wessex Tales* by Thomas Hardy
- *Animal Farm* by George Orwell
- *The Strange Case of Dr Jekyll and Mr Hyde* by Robert Louis Stevenson.

What will this part of the exam consist of?

In the exam you will have to answer **one** question out of two set on the Literary Heritage text you have studied. The first question will always refer to a specific passage, which will be printed on the question paper. The second question will be more general, referring to the text in a wider sense.

How much do I need to know about the background of the set text?

You will **not** be specifically assessed on your knowledge of the social, cultural and historical background of these texts (as required in AO4 in Unit 3). However, it will aid your understanding and enjoyment of the texts if you have considered the times in which they are set. For example, attitudes to marriage and social position in *Pride and Prejudice* are likely to be very different to yours, and some of the beliefs of characters in Hardy's *Wessex Tales* seem absurd and old-fashioned by today's standards.

EXAMINER'S TIPS

Try to ensure you know enough about the historical background of your chosen text to make sense of it, but do not spend a long time researching it in great detail.

Passage-Based Questions

LEARNING CHECKLIST

In this chapter you will learn to:

1 Respond with insight and imagination; select text detail to support interpretations.

2 Explain how the writer uses language, structure and form to present ideas, themes and settings.

Selecting text detail

If you opt to answer the passage-based question in your exam, your main focus should be the given passage, though you should also be able to demonstrate your knowledge and understanding of the text as a whole. You will be marked on your ability to select and comment effectively on relevant quotations from the passage.

Read the extract from *Pride and Prejudice* below.

From *Pride and Prejudice*

by Jane Austen

Mr. Bennet raised his eyes from his book as she entered, and fixed them on her face with a calm unconcern which was not in the least altered by her communication.

'I have not the pleasure of understanding you,' said he, when she had finished her speech. 'Of what are you talking?'

'Of Mr. Collins and Lizzy. Lizzy declares she will not have Mr. Collins, and Mr. Collins begins to say that he will not have Lizzy.'

'And what am I to do on the occasion?—It seems an hopeless business.'

'Speak to Lizzy about it yourself. Tell her that you insist upon her marrying him.'

'Let her be called down. She shall hear my opinion.'

Mrs. Bennet rang the bell, and Miss Elizabeth was summoned to the library.

'Come here, child,' cried her father as she appeared. 'I have sent for you on an affair of importance. I understand that Mr. Collins has made you an offer of marriage. Is it true?' Elizabeth replied that it was. 'Very well—and this offer of marriage you have refused?'

'I have, Sir.'

'Very well. We now come to the point. Your mother insists upon your accepting it. Is it not so, Mrs. Bennet?'

'Yes, or I will never see her again.'

'An unhappy alternative is before you, Elizabeth. From this day you must be a stranger to one of your parents.—Your mother will never see you again if you do *not* marry Mr. Collins, and I will never see you again if you *do*.'

The extract deals with two of the novel's main themes:
1 family relationships
2 marriage.

If you are asked a question about these themes, you need to show your understanding by choosing quotations that illustrate them.

ACTIVITY 1

Which of these quotations are most relevant to marriage? Which are most relevant to family relationships? Explain why. Note that some may be relevant to both.

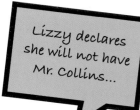
Lizzy declares she will not have Mr. Collins...

And what am I to do on the occasion?—It seems an hopeless business.

Very well—and this offer of marriage you have refused?

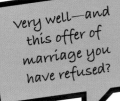
Your mother insists upon your accepting it. Is it not so, Mrs. Bennet?

Tell her that you insist upon her marrying him.

Your mother will never see you again if you do not marry Mr. Collins, and I will never see you again if you do.

ACTIVITY 2

Write two paragraphs: one showing how Austen portrays the idea of marriage in the extract and the other showing how she reveals the relationships within the Bennet family. In each paragraph, include quotations to illustrate your ideas.

EXAMINER'S TIPS

When using quotations in your answer, remember that you should always comment on the significance of your chosen quotation and how this helps to illustrate the point you wish to make.

Evaluating your quotations

When you include quotations in your answer, you need to explain why they are relevant. This means explaining what they say directly, but also looking at what they **suggest**. For example, in the sentence 'All John's driving skills could not prevent the car sliding into the tree,' we are given direct information that there was an accident with John's car hitting a tree. However, the phrase 'all John's driving skills' suggests that he was a good driver, who could usually avoid accidents.

Read this extract from *Silas Marner* by George Eliot.

From *Silas Marner*
by George Eliot

Turning towards the hearth, where the two logs had fallen apart, and sent forth only a red uncertain glimmer, he seated himself on his fireside chair, and was stooping to push his logs together, when, to his blurred vision, it seemed as if there were gold on the floor in front of the hearth. Gold!— his own gold—brought back to him as mysteriously as it had been taken away! He felt his heart begin to beat violently, and for a few moments he was unable to stretch out his hand and grasp the restored treasure.

The heap of gold seemed to glow and get larger beneath his agitated gaze. He leaned forward at last, and stretched forth his hand; but instead of the hard coin with the familiar resisting outline, his fingers encountered soft warm curls. In utter amazement, Silas fell on his knees and bent his head low to examine the marvel: it was a sleeping child—a round, fair thing, with soft yellow rings all over its head. Could this be his little sister come back to him in a dream—his little sister whom he had carried about in his arms for a year before she died, when he was a small boy without shoes or stockings?

The text explains some things directly, but other things are suggested, including references to overall themes and symbols in the novel.

Themes:
1 redemption through love
2 the importance of belief.

Symbols:
1 Silas's short-sightedness
2 his gold
3 the child.

ACTIVITY 3

a Read the following quotations and choose two to focus on.

> Gold!—his own gold—brought back to him as mysteriously as it had been taken away!

> ...it was a sleeping child—a round, fair thing, with soft yellow rings all over its head.

> In utter amazement, Silas fell on his knees and bent his head low to examine the marvel...

> ...his little sister whom he had carried about in his arms for a year before she died, when he was a small boy without shoes or stockings?

> The heap of gold seemed to glow and get larger beneath his agitated gaze.

b Copy and complete the grid below (which has been started with another example), using your two chosen quotations.

QUOTATION	WHAT IT SAYS DIRECTLY	WHAT IT SUGGESTS
'...to his blurred vision it seemed as if there were gold on the floor in front of the hearth.'	Silas mistakes the child's golden hair for his missing treasure.	The child is a gift sent to replace his stolen gold. She is something precious.

c Write a short paragraph for each of your chosen quotations, showing how they illustrate the themes and symbols of the novel. Remember to explain the suggested meaning as well as the direct one.

Interpreting a narrator's viewpoint

The narrator's viewpoint is the perspective from which the story is told; for example, from a first- or third-person perspective. A first-person narrative will be told through the eyes of one person using the pronoun 'I'. A third-person narrative will use pronouns such as 'he', 'she' or 'they', and allows the narrator to be omniscient and able to 'look inside the head' of different characters.

In *Silas Marner*, George Eliot uses a third-person narrative. Read the two extracts from the novel below; the first is about Silas, the second is about Godfrey Cass.

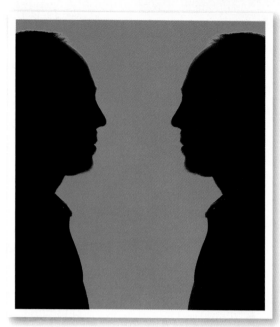

1

From *Silas Marner*
by George Eliot

One day, taking a pair of shoes to be mended, he saw the cobbler's wife seated by the fire, suffering from the terrible symptoms of heart-disease and dropsy, which he had witnessed as the precursors of his mother's death. He felt a rush of pity at the mingled sight and remembrance, and, recalling the relief his mother had found from a simple preparation of foxglove, he promised Sally Oates to bring her something that would ease her, since the doctor did her no good.

2

Still, there was one position worse than the present: it was the position he would be in when the ugly secret was disclosed; and the desire that continually triumphed over every other was that of warding off the evil day, when he would have to bear the consequences of his father's violent resentment for the wound inflicted on his family pride—would have, perhaps, to turn his back on that hereditary ease and dignity which, after all, was a sort of reason for living, and would carry with him the certainty that he was banished for ever from the sight and esteem of Nancy Lammeter.

ACTIVITY 4

a Pick out the verbs in the first extract that tell us how Silas reacted to Sally Oates. How do they contribute to the point of view the author is using?

b In the second extract, pick out the phrases to do with feelings. How do they contribute to the point of view the author is using?

ACTIVITY 5

Write two paragraphs about how George Eliot shows events from different viewpoints in *Silas Marner*. Think about how she shows the differences between the two characters, the language that she uses for each one and what is implied about each character.

Interpreting an author's use of language

A good writer varies his or her language to create particular effects, using a mix of description, dialogue and narration. Read the extract below from *Animal Farm*, which describes what happens immediately after Snowball's expulsion.

From *Animal Farm*
by George Orwell

Silent and terrified, the animals crept back into the barn. In a moment the dogs came bounding back. At first no one had been able to imagine where these creatures came from, but the problem was soon solved: they were the puppies whom Napoleon had taken away from their mothers and reared privately. Though not yet full-grown, they were huge dogs, and as fierce-looking as wolves. They kept close to Napoleon. It was noticed that they wagged their tails to him in the same way as the other dogs had been used to do to Mr. Jones.

ACTIVITY 6

With a partner, answer these questions, referring to words and phrases from the extract.

a What does the description of the animals in the first sentence tell us about them?

b What does Napoleon's name tell the reader about him?

c What is suggested by Napoleon having taken the puppies away some time before?

d What effect is created by the description of the dogs?

e What is implied by the way the dogs wag their tails?

f How does the final sentence foreshadow later events in the novel?

ACTIVITY 7

Write a paragraph about the way George Orwell uses language to create effects in this extract. You should think about:

- adjectives and verbs
- comparisons, including simile
- name choice
- variety in sentence length and structure.

EXAMINER'S TIPS

Before you write your response to the passage-based question, make a short **plan**. Begin by annotating the passage and then group your points into linked sections. Use your plan to decide how you will order these sections in your response.

How language supports ideas, themes and settings

The **way** an author writes is as important as **what** he or she writes. A good reader can identify how the writer uses words, phrases and sentences to create effects that engage the reader. For example, long sentences and detailed descriptions slow the pace of reading and help to create images in the reader's mind. Alternatively, short phrases and strong verbs listed closely together increase the pace and level of excitement for the reader.

Read the two short extracts below from *Lord of the Flies* which describe how Simon is killed. Think carefully about which one is slower and more descriptive and which one is faster-paced and more exciting.

1

At once the crowd surged after it, poured down the rock, leapt onto the beast, screamed, struck, bit, tore. There were no words, and no movements but the tearing of teeth and claws.

2

Softly, surrounded by a fringe of inquisitive bright creatures, itself a silver shape beneath the steadfast constellations, Simon's dead body moved out towards the open sea.

Both extracts link to the theme of good and evil in the novel, looking at
1 savagery versus civilization
2 innocence versus corruption.

The setting begins as a paradise but quickly turns into a hell. The author uses the symbolism of dark and light to represent evil/ignorance and goodness/truth.

ACTIVITY 8

a Using a copy of the extracts, highlight all the verbs in each one. Which one has more?

b Use a different colour to highlight all the adjectives in the two extracts. Which one has more?

ACTIVITY 9

Work with a partner to complete the grid.

WORDS OR PHRASES	RELATIONSHIP TO IDEAS, THEMES AND SETTING
'screamed, struck, bit, tore'	These verbs are very violent, suggesting the boys' fear and aggression as they set upon Simon. They are becoming like savages or like the beast that Simon said was 'only us'. In a deeper sense, they are losing their innocence.
'the tearing of teeth and claws'	
'inquisitive, bright creatures'	
'the steadfast constellations'	

Another way in which authors use language to support the ideas, themes and setting of a text is through dialogue. Look at the extract from *Lord of the Flies* on the right.

What characters say and do informs you about their personalities and motivations, but it can also move the plot forward and support the themes, ideas and setting. The conversation between Ralph, Piggy and Simon is relevant to the themes of savagery versus civilization, law and order versus chaos, and reason versus instinct, in a setting where the 'population' is at war with itself.

From *Lord of the Flies*
by William Golding

Simon stirred in the dark.

'Go on being chief.'

'You shut up, young Simon! Why couldn't you say there wasn't a beast?'

'I'm scared of him,' said Piggy, 'and that's why I know him. If you're scared of someone you hate him but you can't stop thinking about him. You kid yourself he's all right really, an' then when you see him again; it's like asthma an' you can't breathe. I tell you what. He hates you too, Ralph –'

'Me? Why me?'

'I dunno. You got him over the fire; an' you're chief an' he isn't.'

'But he's, he's, Jack Merridew!'

'I been in bed so much I done some thinking. I know about people. I know about me. And him. He can't hurt you: but if you stand out of the way he'd hurt the next thing. And that's me.'

'Piggy's right, Ralph. There's you and Jack. Go on being chief.'

ACTIVITY 10

Copy and complete this spider diagram. Add relevant dialogue from the extract above to each 'leg'. Explain how it relates to the theme, idea or setting.

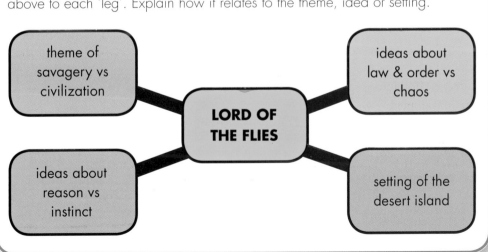

ACTIVITY 11

Write four paragraphs, using your spider diagram as a plan, showing how Golding uses dialogue in the extract to support the themes, ideas and setting.

LEARNING CHECKLIST

In this chapter you will learn to:

1 Respond with insight and imagination; select text detail to support interpretations.

2 Explain how the writer uses language, structure and form to present ideas, themes and settings.

AO1 & AO2

UNIT 4

Interpreting an author's meaning

When you interpret any text, you need to show first that you understand what the author is trying to say. This means not just understanding the direct surface meaning, but also what the author **implies**. This skill is sometimes referred to as 'reading between the lines'.

Read the extract below from *The Strange Case of Dr Jekyll and Mr Hyde*. Then read the student response on the right, which shows an understanding of implied as well as direct meaning.

From *The Strange Case of Dr Jekyll and Mr Hyde*
by Robert Louis Stevenson

All at once, I saw two figures: one a little man who was stumping along eastward at a good walk, and the other a girl of maybe eight or ten who was running as hard as she was able down a cross street. Well, sir, the two ran into one another naturally enough at the corner; and then came the horrible part of the thing; for the man trampled calmly over the child's body and left her screaming on the ground.

STUDENT

Stevenson uses the incident of Mr Hyde trampling over the child to introduce a character who has no conscience. This is shown in the use of the word 'calmly' as though his action was unimportant to him. His refusal to stop and see if she is hurt shows someone who is totally self-centred. The phrase 'a little man' implies that he is small in moral outlook as well as stature.

ACTIVITY I

'Utterson, I swear to God,' cried the doctor, 'I swear to God I will never set eyes on him again. I bind my honour to you that I am done with him in this world. It is all at an end. And indeed he does not want my help; you do not know him as I do; he is safe, he is quite safe; mark my words, he will never more be heard of.'

a Discuss any words or phrases from the extract above that imply something deeper than what is directly said.

b Write a paragraph giving your opinion of what the author is telling us about Dr Jekyll and his relationship with Mr Hyde in this extract.

Interpreting an author's purpose

Most good story writers have something important to say about life or society. This message is the main theme or **purpose** of the story. In her novel *Pride and Prejudice*, Jane Austen explores the dangers of the words given in the title. George Orwell shows how power corrupts in *Animal Farm*. In *Lord of the Flies*, William Golding reveals how primitive instinct can triumph over rational laws. In 'The Withered Arm', Thomas Hardy uses country superstitions to highlight the destructive effects of the desire for revenge.

As a reader, you have to look for clues that will reveal the author's purpose. In 'The Withered Arm', we are given clues that Rhoda Brook has not forgiven Farmer Lodge for leaving her and that she feels resentful towards his new wife. By the time she realizes she is fond of Gertrude, it is too late and the effect of her 'overlooking' destroys them all.

ACTIVITY 2

Copy the grid below. With a partner, look at these events from 'The Withered Arm' and decide what they reveal about Hardy's **purpose**. Choose a quotation to support each point.

EVENT	WHAT THIS REVEALS ABOUT HARDY'S PURPOSE	QUOTATION AS EVIDENCE
first mention of Rhoda		
Rhoda gives her son instructions about the new wife		
Rhoda's dream about Gertrude		
Farmer Lodge's reaction to the withering arm		
the visit to Conjuror Trendle		
the scene with the hanged man		

ACTIVITY 3

Write two paragraphs giving your views about what Hardy wanted his readers to learn from this story. Comment on what he is saying about the human mind, about superstition and about social class. Remember to use quotations to back up your points.

Identifying key events in the novel

In order to explain the structure and form of a story, you need to have a good overview of the whole text. One way of making sure this is clear in your mind is to draw up a storyboard. This is a summary of a story shown through pictures and captions. You can also include important quotations.

Creating a storyboard can help you to identify the key events in the story and help you to analyse the **plot**. Think about how the events are sequenced. How much time passes between the key events? Does time speed up or slow down in places? What is the effect of this?

ACTIVITY 4

a With a partner, draw up a storyboard for your chosen text.
- Use a grid like the one started below for *Lord of the Flies*.
- Identify what you think are the six most important events in the story.
- Sketch out those events and include captions.
- Add some quotations to link to your chosen events.

(1)

We're having a meeting. Come and join in.

(2) The boys all meet for the first time

(3)

(4)

(5)

(6)

b Do you notice anything interesting about how these events are sequenced?

Analysing plot structure

Most novels follow one of two main types of **plot structure**:

1 **linear** – where the story progresses from the beginning to the end, with events described in chronological order.

2 **non-linear** – where events in the story are not arranged in chronological order, but are revealed through techniques such as flashbacks or through clues that hint at what is to come.

In addition to the **sequence** of events, authors can also introduce **parallels** into their narratives. This is where certain events in the story deliberately reflect others in the plot.

An example of a novel with a linear plot is *Pride and Prejudice. Lord of the Flies*, on the other hand, is non-linear. *Animal Farm* includes a striking parallel in the narrative, in which the beginning closely reflects the ending. At the beginning of the novel the animals are oppressed by humans; at the end of the novel they are oppressed by the pigs. Orwell uses this parallel to make a point about how those in power are easily tempted into corruption.

ACTIVITY 5

Read the following extracts from *Animal Farm*. The first is taken from the beginning of the novel and the second is taken from the end. With a partner discuss how Orwell creates parallels between each point in the narrative.

1 Let us face it: our lives are miserable, laborious and short. We are born, we are given just so much food as will keep the breath in our bodies, and those of us who are capable of it are forced to work to the last atom of our strength.

2 They [the animals] were generally hungry, they slept on straw, they drank from the pool, they laboured in the fields; in winter they were troubled by the cold, and in the summer by the flies.

ACTIVITY 6

a Put these events from *Animal Farm* in the order in which they happen:
- the false confessions and the executions of pigs, hens, sheep and others
- the dispatch of Boxer to the knacker's yard
- the battle of the cowshed
- the pigs walking on their hind legs
- Old Major's speech
- drinks and card games with farmers
- the battle after the windmill is blown up.

b Decide whether *Animal Farm* is a linear or non-linear narrative.

c Can you identify any other parallels between the events of the novel? What do they reveal?

ACTIVITY 7

With a partner, copy and complete the grid below. Use your order of events from Activity 6 in the first column. Discuss possible answers before completing the other two columns.

EVENT	ACTIONS THAT CAUSED THE EVENT	HOW ACTIONS AND EVENTS RELATE TO THE THEMES, IDEAS & SETTING
Old Major's speech about freedom and equality. He sees Man as the enemy.	Mr Jones's drunken neglect of Manor Farm and Old Major's knowledge that he will soon die.	The <u>idea</u> of a future where animals would get the benefits of their work and would live as equals, sharing everything. The <u>theme</u> of freedom from oppression. The <u>setting</u> makes it possible for the whole community to be present at the speech.

ACTIVITY 8

Use your grid to write three paragraphs.
a Describe the structure of the novel.
b Say how this structure helps to show themes and ideas in the novel.
c Show how this structure links to the setting of the novel.

UNIT 4

Interpreting an author's use of setting

The **setting** of a novel or story involves the place, the time and the situation. In *Pride and Prejudice*, the setting is a country village at the beginning of the 19th century and the situation involves a family of girls and their efforts to make suitable marriages. Austen uses this small, enclosed society to reveal private relationships within a family.

From *Pride and Prejudice*
by Jane Austen

The village of Longbourn was only one mile from Meryton; a most convenient distance for the young ladies, who were usually tempted thither three or four times a week, to pay their duty to their aunt and to a milliner's shop just over the way. The two youngest of the family, Catherine and Lydia, were particularly frequent in these attentions; their minds were more vacant than their sisters', and when nothing better offered, a walk to Meryton was necessary to amuse their morning hours and furnish conversation for the evening; and however bare of news the country in general might be, they always contrived to learn some from their aunt. At present, indeed, they were well supplied both with news and happiness by the recent arrival of a militia regiment in the neighbourhood; it was to remain the whole winter, and Meryton was the head quarters.

ACTIVITY 9

- duty to their aunt and to a milliner's shop
- amuse their morning hours
- a most convenient distance
- contrived to learn some from their aunt
- when nothing better offered
- a militia regiment in the neighbourhood
- well supplied both with news and happiness
- to remain the whole winter

Copy the quotations in the speech bubbles above into the first column of a grid. In the second column, next to each quotation, write what you think Jane Austen is telling us about her setting, and how it affects family relationships and characters.

EXTENSION TASK

Write a paragraph giving your interpretation of the way in which Jane Austen uses setting in this extract, considering the precise language she uses.

LITERARY HERITAGE PROSE

How should I prepare for the exam?

The best, and most obvious, way of preparing yourself for the exam on your prose text is to make sure that you **read it carefully** and **understand it fully**.

What does 'read it carefully' mean?

This means two things:

- When you first read the text, try to do so in extended periods of perhaps an hour at a time, rather than reading it in short, distracted bursts. You need to read a long text with concentration, without constantly stopping; for instance, to chat to a friend or to send a text message.
- Second, when you feel you really know the prose text, keep it fresh in your mind by picking it up from time to time and re-reading part of it for perhaps 15 minutes. Try to do this regularly, re-reading a different part each time.

What does 'understand it fully' mean?

In order to ensure that you 'understand it fully', your first reading of the text should be to find out what happens and what the main characters do. Your second reading gives you the chance to pay more attention to detail. It's a good idea to check the meanings of particular words and phrases that you are not sure of. You might regret not doing so if they appear in a passage the examiner has chosen for the exam!

EXAMINER'S TIPS

- ✔ You will gain marks by commenting on the **structure** of the text. If you choose to answer a passage-based question, you should consider the structure of the passage as well as how that passage fits within the wider structure of the whole text.
- ✔ Don't try to compare this text with another you may have read. Comparison is not required in this part of the exam.

What else should I bear in mind?

Preparing for the exam includes careful **revision** in the days leading up to the exam. Try to re-read the text. If you feel you already know it well, skim-read some pages. After all, it doesn't now require the concentration it took when you read it for the first and second times. Knowing the text well is vital.

See the film version

You may find it very useful to see a film version of the text you are going to be examined on. There are film versions available of most of the texts, though while most follow the text fairly closely, some do not. For example, the 1954 animated film version of *Animal Farm* ends with the rest of the animals defeating the pigs.

Remember you are being examined on the **text**, not the film, so do ensure you are aware of any differences!

Read the question carefully

You will certainly have written timed practice essays during the term, but in the exam, remember to answer the question on the paper **in front of you** and not one you have practised previously.

Source text 4.1

JANE AUSTEN: *Pride and Prejudice*

The idea of Mr. Collins, with all his solemn composure, being run away with by his feelings, made Elizabeth so near laughing that she could not use the short pause he allowed in any attempt to stop him farther, and he continued:

'My reasons for marrying are, first, that I think it a right thing for every clergyman in easy circumstances (like myself) to set the example of matrimony in his parish. Secondly, that I am convinced it will add very greatly to my happiness; and thirdly—which perhaps I ought to have mentioned earlier, that it is the particular advice and recommendation of the very noble lady whom I have the honour of calling patroness. Twice has she condescended to give me her opinion (unasked too!) on this subject; and it was but the very Saturday night before I left Hunsford—between our pools at quadrille, while Mrs. Jenkinson was arranging Miss de Bourgh's foot-stool, that she said, "Mr. Collins, you must marry. A clergyman like you must marry.—Chuse properly, chuse a gentlewoman for *my* sake; and for your *own*, let her be an active, useful sort of person, not brought up high, but able to make a small income go a good way. This is my advice. Find such a woman as soon as you can, bring her to Hunsford, and I will visit her." Allow me, by the way, to observe, my fair cousin, that I do not reckon the notice and kindness of Lady Catherine de Bourgh as among the least of the advantages in my power to offer. You will find her manners beyond any thing I can describe; and your wit and vivacity I think must be acceptable to her, especially when tempered with the silence and respect which her rank will inevitably excite. Thus much for my general intention in favour of matrimony; it remains to be told why my views were directed to Longbourn instead of my own neigbourhood, where I assure you there are many amiable young women. But the fact is, that being, as I am, to inherit this estate after the death of your honoured father, (who, however, may live many years longer,) I could not satisfy myself without resolving to chuse a wife from among his daughters, that the loss to them might be as little as possible, when the melancholy event takes place—which, however, as I have already said, may

5

10

15

20

25

31

Source text 4.1 continued

not be for several years. This has been my motive, my fair cousin, and I flatter   30
myself it will not sink me in your esteem. And now nothing remains for me but
to assure you in the most animated language of the violence of my affection.
To fortune I am perfectly indifferent, and shall make no demand of that nature
on your father, since I am well aware that it could not be complied with; and
that one thousand pounds in the 4 per cents, which will not be yours until   35
after your mother's decease, is all that you may ever be entitled to. On that
head, therefore, I shall be uniformly silent; and you may assure yourself that
no ungenerous reproach shall ever pass my lips when we are married.'

Sample task 4.1

1a Why do you think Elizabeth turns down this proposal of marriage?   [24]

EXAMINER'S TIPS

If you choose to answer the passage-based
question, remember to focus your answer closely
on the passage provided on the exam paper. It is
helpful to make some reference to the whole text
to demonstrate your understanding; however, do
make sure most of your response relates to the
passage specifically.

immediate focus on question

Perhaps the first reason for Elizabeth turning down Mr Collins's proposal here is that he does not mention that he loves her, though he does refer to 'the violence' of his 'affection'. Love does not seem to matter to Mr Collins, since he has known Elizabeth only a matter of days, and he is able to propose to, and be accepted by, Charlotte Lucas soon after. As we see in the novel, love does matter to Elizabeth and she shows every sign of being in a very happy marriage at the end of the novel.

shows awareness of whole novel

Mrs Bennet is very keen to get her daughters married, preferably to men with money. For a woman at that time, marriage meant stability. Mrs Bennet is in favour of Mr Collins's proposal, as she shows when Elizabeth is trying to avoid being alone in the room with Mr Collins: 'Lizzy, I insist upon your staying and hearing Mr. Collins.'

suitable quotation

Mr Collins, as I said, doesn't mention 'love' in his proposal. The 'violence of my affection' doesn't sound romantic.

identifies a key reason: lack of romance

Mr Collins gives a number of unromantic reasons for proposing to Lizzy. First he says it's a clergyman's job to 'set the example of matrimony in his parish', meaning he is marrying to encourage others to do. Secondly he says that 'matrimony' will make him happy as 'it will add very greatly to my happiness'. He has nothing to say about what matrimony will add to Lizzy's happiness. He also says he was advised to do so by Lady Catherine, which suggests that he is proposing to keep on Lady Catherine's good side.

shows perception and insight into what is NOT said

Mr Collins is following Lady Catherine's advice and he doesn't seem to understand how patronizing she is being to

Student response 4.1 continued

Mr Collins's future wife when she describes her as 'an active useful sort of person'. By repeating this to Lizzy, he seems to be too stupid to realize that he is insulting her. He makes matters worse by saying Lizzy's wit and vivacity must be 'tempered with silence and respect', not understanding that wit and vivacity can't be seen if you are silent!

> *quotation embedded with fluency*

Mr Collins is a tactless man who obviously thinks that Lizzy will be as blinded as he is by Lady Catherine, who comes through here, as she does later in the novel, as an unpleasant snob. Another reason for proposing to Lizzy is that the 'entailment' means he will inherit the estate when Mr Bennet dies. Mentioning the future death of a girl's father in a proposal is not very romantic. Worse is the fact that he mentions it twice and sounds regretful that he might have to wait several years before Mr Bennet has the goodness to die! Also he seems to rub Lizzy's nose in the fact that she is fairly poor, saying that he will be 'uniformly silent' about it when they are married, though he implies he might be thinking about it even if he says nothing.

> *shows good insight*

> *expression rather informal*

Jane Austen makes this an unattractive proposal to both Lizzy and the reader, and Mr Collins deserves to be rejected.

> *shows clear under-standing*

EXAMINER'S COMMENTS OCR

- This shows some critical engagement with Mr Collins's proposal and some insight into how Austen makes it unattractive to Lizzy.
- Understanding of Mr Collins's character is clear throughout.
- Good consistent focus on responding to the question, showing insight and perception.
- This is a strong top-band response.

EXAMINER'S TIPS

Don't spend time writing details about the writer's background or any other books he or she has written. Such details are rarely, if ever, required by the question.

Sample task 4.2

GEORGE ORWELL: *Animal Farm*

The animals give Boxer the award 'Animal Hero, First Class'. In what ways, do you think, does he deserve it?

Remember to support your ideas with details from the novel. [15]

Student response 4.2

In Animal Farm, Boxer is a cart-horse. He is very strong and works very hard on the farm. In Chapter 1 he is described as 'an enormous beast, nearly eighteen hands high, and as strong as any two ordinary horses put together'. He is very strong, but 'a white stripe down his nose gave him a somewhat stupid appearance' and he 'was not a first-rate intelligence'. In Animal Farm the animals respect him 'for his steadiness of character and tremendous powers of work'. The animals give him the award 'Animal Hero, First Class' for helping to drive away Jones and his men at the Battle of the Cowshed. This doesn't stop the pigs selling him to the knackers when he is no longer useful to them. Boxer's lack of intelligence is shown when he tries to learn the letters of the alphabet. He can't remember what comes after the letter D. I think he makes up for his lack of intelligence by being so useful on the farm. I don't think the animals would have won the Battle of the Cowshed without Snowball and Boxer.

good use of quotation

not really relevant

again, not really relevant to the question

shows knowledge of the context

selects relevant detail

Student response 4.2 continued

Snowball is the brains and Boxer has the strength to frighten the men. 'But the most terrifying spectacle of all was Boxer, rearing up on his hind legs and striking out with his great iron-shod hoofs like a stallion. His very first blow took a stable-lad from Foxwood on the skull and stretched him lifeless in the mud. At the sight, several men dropped their sticks and tried to run.' So you can see that Boxer was very important at the Battle of the Cowshed because the men ran away when they saw what he can do. It is because of what they did at the Battle that both Snowball and Boxer are made Animal Heroes, First Class. Boxer is really a gentle giant. He is very sorry to have killed the stable-lad and even has tears in his eyes. The stable-lad isn't dead, so Boxer must have been pleased that he didn't really kill him.

I think that Boxer deserves his medal for the way he works so hard for the animals. When Snowball is chased off the farm, Napoleon steals his plans and the animals start to build the windmill. This is very hard work and I don't think they would have been able to build the windmill without Boxer. It says, 'Nothing could have been achieved without Boxer, whose strength seemed equal to that of all the rest of the animals put together.' He has two slogans, 'I will work harder' and 'Napoleon is always right'. He does work harder and harder, but we find out that he is wrong about Napoleon when Napoleon and the pigs get money for his body when the knacker takes him away.

(Margin annotations:)

overlong quotation

textual detail to support comment

this part of the quote is relevant

good explanation

good development of response

lack of focus here

.....I think Boxer deserves his award for the way he fights at the .....
Battle of the Windmill when Fredericks, who stands for
Germany in the book, blows up the windmill. The animals fight
the men and 'Three of them had their heads broken by blows from
Boxer's hoofs'.

hints at Orwell's satire

missed opportunity to comment on language

.....He deserves his award when the animals have to rebuild the .....
windmill. Boxer is not as strong as he was. Although he is old, he
'did not care what happened so long as a good store of stone was ..
accumulated before he went on pension'.

developing response using quotation

.....So I think Boxer deserved his medal. He didn't deserve to be .....
treated as he was at the end by the pigs.

EXAMINER'S COMMENTS OCR
RECOGNISING ACHIEVEMENT

- This is a response that focuses quite well on the question and selects relevant textual detail to support the interpretation.

- There is awareness of the time-span of the novel, from Boxer being in his prime to his weakness at the end.

- There is personal response to both Boxer and the pigs.

- This response is within the middle band.

EXAMINER'S TIPS OCR
RECOGNISING ACHIEVEMENT

Try to make sure that everything you include in your response is relevant to the question.

HOW TO APPROACH UNIT 4

CONTEMPORARY POETRY

What will this part of the exam consist of?

In this section you will need to answer **one** question.

The question can be **either**

- on one of the six set contemporary poets

or

- on a single unseen poem (that you have not previously studied).

Here are the six set poets, **one** of whom you might choose to study:

- Simon Armitage
- Carol-Ann Duffy
- Gillian Clarke
- Seamus Heaney
- Wendy Cope
- Benjamin Zephaniah.

What will the questions be like?

If you choose to answer a question on a **set poet**, you will have a choice of three questions. The first question will be on a poem printed on the question paper. The second and third questions will ask you to comment on, criticize and analyse **one** poem from a choice of two poems by the poet you have studied.

If you choose to answer a question on an **unseen poem**, the poem will be printed on the question paper and you will be asked to comment on, criticize and analyse it. If you are particularly lucky, it might be a poem that you have previously come across in preparation for the exam and in your own wider reading!

What is contemporary poetry?

Contemporary poetry is poetry written by poets alive today. They often write about recent and current events and issues. For example, Simon Armitage's poem 'The Convergence of the Twain' is about the crashing of aircraft into New York's World Trade Centre on 11th September 2001. Gillian Clarke's 'On The Train' touches on the fear of train crashes like the one at Hatfield in the year 2000.

Before you start your studies your teacher will decide with you whether you will study one of the set contemporary poets or concentrate on learning skills that would help you to write with understanding about almost any contemporary poem you might come across.

LEARNING CHECKLIST

In this chapter you will learn to:

1 Respond with insight and imagination; select text detail to support interpretations.

2 Explain how the writer uses language, structure and form to present ideas, themes and settings.

Reading and responding to poetry

Poetry is like chocolate: it is very rich and intense. Poets choose their words with great care to help you visualize the images they wish to convey and to inspire you to think more deeply about the ideas they raise. Responding to poetry is about using your own imagination to appreciate what is written. When you read a good poem carefully, it should have an effect on you. You may find things that move you or make you smile. Remember that responding to a poem is personal, so not everyone will react in the same way.

The diagram below suggests things to consider when reading a poem.

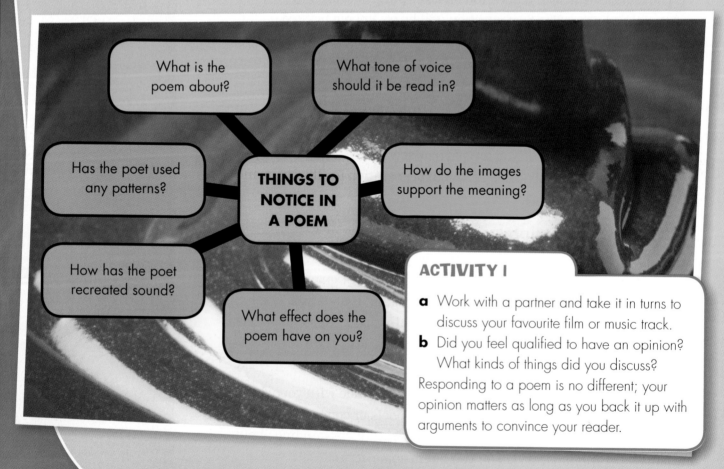

What is the poem about?

What tone of voice should it be read in?

Has the poet used any patterns?

THINGS TO NOTICE IN A POEM

How do the images support the meaning?

How has the poet recreated sound?

What effect does the poem have on you?

ACTIVITY I

a Work with a partner and take it in turns to discuss your favourite film or music track.

b Did you feel qualified to have an opinion? What kinds of things did you discuss?

Responding to a poem is no different; your opinion matters as long as you back it up with arguments to convince your reader.

How poets choose words

In your exam you will be expected to comment on the specific words that the poet uses.

ACTIVITY 2

a Imagine you are writing the poem on the right. Decide which words you would use to fill the gaps.

b Read out your version of the poem. Look at Heaney's version in your Anthology and compare your choices to his.

c What do you notice about the words Heaney chose? Do you notice anything about the rhyme patterns?

From 'Blackberry-Picking'
by Seamus Heaney

Late August, given heavy rain and _____

For a full week, the blackberries would ripen.

At first, just one, a glossy purple clot

Among others, _____, _____, hard as a _____.

You ate that first one and its flesh was sweet

Like _____ _____: summer's blood was in it

Leaving stains upon the tongue and _____ for

Picking. Then red ones _____ up and that hunger

Sent us out with milk-cans, pea-tins, jam-pots

Where briars scratched and wet grass _____ our boots.

Round hayfields, cornfields and potato-drills

We trekked and picked until the cans were full,

Until the _____ bottom had been covered

With green ones, and on top big dark _____ burned

Like a _____ __ _____. Our hands were peppered

With thorn pricks, our palms sticky as _____.

Connotations are the extra associations that words have for readers, alongside their dictionary definitions. For example, words such as 'scratched', 'burned' and the image of 'a plate of eyes' all convey a hostile, rather threatening, atmosphere and tone. The mention of blood and clots carry connotations about injury and death. Heaney is preparing us for the second stanza by suggesting, through connotation, that something will go wrong.

131

Understanding imagery

It is not just poets who use metaphors. Ever been 'gutted'? Well, literally that means to have your intestines removed, but we use it to say we are really upset about something. We say he/she has 'a face like thunder' when someone looks angry and that a person who is not paying attention has their 'head in the clouds'. Poets often make up their own images allowing them to convey their feelings in a way that is both individual and precise. Gillian Clarke's poem, 'My Box' is a love poem dedicated to her husband and the life they have shared together.

ACTIVITY 3

Read 'My Box' in your Anthology and underline all the words that make the box sound precious. What does the box represent metaphorically? What does it reveal about the writer's feelings?

ACTIVITY 4

Write your own poem called 'My Box'.

a In the first stanza, describe the box you would like to put all your favourite things into. It might be a handmade wooden box like Clarke's, or maybe a titanium box with a combination lock, or a gold casket studded with precious stones. Include where you got it from or who made it for you.

b In your second stanza, write about all the things you would put in your box. They have to be specific things; for example, instead of just 'a sunset' make it detailed, like 'the sunset over the River Mersey in autumn'.

c In your last stanza, write about where you keep your box and what might happen to it in later years.

EXAMINER'S TIPS

Poets will often deliberately use metaphors and similes that suggest a number of meanings and emotions Rather than looking for one meaning, think about how these features work to create a variety of impressions.

Reading the clues

Poets often speak indirectly to their readers. Instead of giving straightforward information, they give clues and ideas, leaving readers to build up their own pictures.

In the panels below are some quotations from 'About His Person' by Simon Armitage. This poem depicts a man and an event, just by noting things that the man carries and the appearance of his hands.

ACTIVITY 5

If a stranger were to look in your schoolbag, what would they find out about you? Discuss with a partner.

a rolled up note of explanation

A brace of keys

an analogue watch, self-winding, stopped

a pocket-size diary slashed with a pencil

A giveaway photograph stashed in his wallet

a ring of white unweathered skin

Five pounds fifty in change, exactly

ACTIVITY 6

Using the quotations above, write a brief description of the person who owns these things. You might find it easiest to jot down your thoughts on a spider diagram like the one below.

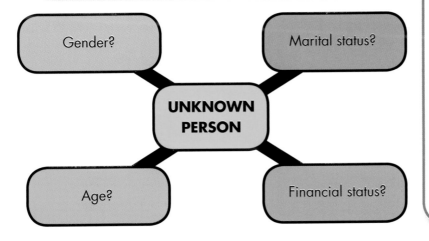

ACTIVITY 7

a Read the complete poem 'About His Person' in your Anthology. Check whether your ideas were on the right lines.

b Using a copy, highlight words that suggest death or endings; for example, 'expiry'. What do you think was the fate of this man? What hints can you find in the poem to suggest why this may have happened?

c Look at the line endings. What is Armitage doing with **form** (the pattern of words and lines)?

Interpreting the poet's subject matter: experiences of school

School is an experience shared by most people. Although this experience has changed a little since Carol-Ann Duffy went to school in the 1960s, you will recognize many of the things she includes in her poems. 'In Mrs Tilscher's Class' is about primary school and 'The Good Teachers' is about secondary school.

At that time, children at primary school were given small bottles of milk at break, teachers wrote with chalk and bells were old-fashioned ones rung by hand. Brady and Hindley were notorious child murderers convicted in 1966. News of the murders sparked panic among parents, who feared for the safety of their children.

ACTIVITY 8

Read 'In Mrs Tilscher's Class' in your Anthology.
a Why might Duffy have chosen to write the poem in the second person?
b In the first stanza, do you think the children understand what they are learning?
c In the second stanza, how does Duffy show her positive attitudes towards school?
d Why do you think Duffy refers to Brady and Hindley in the second stanza?
e How are the tadpoles relevant to the main themes of the poem?
f How does Mrs Tilscher finally disappoint Duffy?
g How does Duffy use language to appeal to the senses?

During Duffy's schooldays, secondary school was much more formal than it is now and the teachers were often very aloof and strict. The school described in 'The Good Teachers' seems to be a girls' school from which the speaker longs to escape.

ACTIVITY 9

Read 'The Good Teachers' in your Anthology.
a The speaker in this poem is rather rebellious. How does Duffy suggest this through her word choices?
b How is the pupil contrasted with the teachers in the poem?

Parody

A **parody** is a humorous imitation of the style of someone or something. Some poets use parody to write new, amusing poems in which the originals are still recognizable.

Read the poems below. The poem on the left is the popular Victorian poem by Jane Taylor. The poem on the right is a parody of it by Lewis Carroll. Notice how Carroll has retained the rhythm of the original as well as some of the words and rhyme patterns, but he has changed the subject to a more comic one.

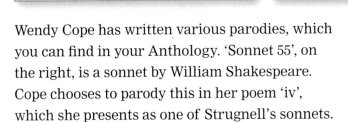

Twinkle, twinkle, little star,
How I wonder what you are!
Up above the world so high,
Like a diamond in the sky.

Twinkle, twinkle, little bat!
How I wonder what you're at!
Up above the world you fly,
Like a tea-tray in the sky.

Wendy Cope has written various parodies, which you can find in your Anthology. 'Sonnet 55', on the right, is a sonnet by William Shakespeare. Cope chooses to parody this in her poem 'iv', which she presents as one of Strugnell's sonnets.

Who is Strugnell?

In her 'Strugnell' sonnets, Cope uses an invented bad poet called James Strugnell as her narrator. Using this narrator, Cope parodies the process of composing poetry itself. She writes these poems as if he had composed them. Strugnell's name even sounds rather like 'struggle', which highlights his incompetence as a writer.

ACTIVITY 10

Look at 'From Strugnell's Sonnets (iv)' in your Anthology.

a How has Cope changed the words but kept the rhyme and rhythm to create humour in her poem? Make a list of all the changes.

b Has Cope changed the meaning of the poem? How has it moved from being a serious poem to a parody?

'Sonnet 55'
by William Shakespeare

Not marble, nor the gilded monuments
Of princes shall outlive this pow'rful rhyme,
But you shall shine more bright in these contents
Than unswept stone besmeared with sluttish time.
When wasteful war shall statues overturn,
And broils root out the work of masonry,
Nor Mars his sword, nor war's quick fire shall burn
The living record of your memory.
'Gainst death, and all oblivious enmity
Shall you pace forth, your praise shall still find room,
Even in the eyes of all posterity
That wear this world out to the ending doom.
So, till the judgment that yourself arise,
You live in this, and dwell in lovers' eyes.

Anthology: Analysing Poetry

AO1 & AO2

LEARNING CHECKLIST

In this chapter you will learn to:

1 Respond with insight and imagination; select text detail to support interpretations.

2 Explain how the writer uses language, structure and form to present ideas, themes and settings.

Themes in poetry

Poetry is often used to express abstract ideas, and behind each subject there is often a theme. For example, Seamus Heaney's poem 'Follower' is about being a small boy wanting to be like his father, but beyond this subject matter, one of the main **themes** in the poem is the cycle of life. The subject of Duffy's 'Dream of a Lost Friend' is nightmare, but its theme is bereavement.

ACTIVITY I

The quotations in the boxes below are from poems that appear in your Anthology. Match them up to the relevant themes listed beneath.

1 '…the star goes out in its eye'

2 'a ring of white unweathered skin.'

3 'Between my finger and my thumb/The squat pen rests./ I'll dig with it.'

4 'You roll the waistband/ of your skirt over and over, all leg, all/dumb insolence, smoke-rings.'

5 'the inky tadpoles changed/from commas into exclamation marks'

6 'I've never dreamt of being white/But I can't bear being abused'

7 'I hear your words,/they play inside my head like broken chords.'

prejudice   death   rebellion

growing up   arguing   writing poetry   divorce

Using poetry to protest

Poets are passionate about things that matter to them and poetry is a great way to express protest. To make an effective point, poets will use repetition to drum a point home, and rhymes to make the message stick in the reader's mind. The letters **p**, **d** and **b** are strong consonants. These sounds can be used to lend weight to an argument. If you think about some angry words in the English language, you will see why.

In 'Bought and Sold', Benjamin Zephaniah complains about the way writers seem to be easily tamed by the lure of fame. Over the course of his career, Zephaniah himself has turned down many honours.

ACTIVITY 2

a Read the poem 'Bought and Sold' in your Anthology and, using a copy, underline all the negative words. What effect do they have on you?

b Label the rhyme scheme. How does this pattern and structure add to the impact of the poem?

c List all the words that include **p**, **b** or **d** sounds. Write a brief paragraph explaining why you think Zephaniah chooses to use these words.

EXAMINER'S TIPS

Poets often craft their poems so that features such as rhyme, rhythm, language choice and stanza structure work together to create an impact on the reader. When analysing poetry consider how features work collectively to create an overall impression.

In 'Having a Word', Zephaniah questions the jargon that is associated with politics, society and human rights. He asks the reader to think more deeply about whether these words reflect reality.

ACTIVITY 3

a Read 'Having a Word' in your Anthology. In this poem, Zephaniah uses words derived from Latin: **equality**, **democracy**, **liberation** and **security**. Find out what these words mean.

b Why do you think Zephaniah chooses to use them?

c **Black English** is a variety of English which comes from a fusion of languages. Zephaniah uses Black English words like 'dis', 'dread' and 'folk' in 'Chant of a Homesick Nigga'. Read this poem in you Anthology. Why do you think he has chosen to write in this dialect?

Reading between the lines

Wendy Cope is a poet who likes to have fun with words. In 'Lonely Hearts' and 'Reading Scheme', she uses a form called a **villanelle**. This form is characterized by the repetition of lines which occur at the end of alternate stanzas and at the end of the poem. Cope uses this form to poke fun at the repetitive nature of lonely hearts advertisements and books from reading schemes, designed to teach young children how to read.

'Reading Scheme' is funny because Cope has managed to construct a narrative very different to the cosy stereotypes found in real children's books. On the surface everything sounds fine, but reading between the lines reveals a different story. 'The milkman likes Mummy. She likes them all' implies that 'Mummy' is unfaithful, and not only with the milkman. Jane and Peter are spying on them when 'Daddy' returns home unexpectedly and 'looks very cross'. He may have a gun. The milkman makes a rapid getaway over the wall.

ACTIVITY 4

Re-read 'Reading Scheme' in your Anthology with a partner. On a copy, highlight all the phrases that have a double meaning. Write a headline for a gossip magazine based on the poem.

ACTIVITY 5

a Read 'Lonely Hearts' in your Anthology. Then find relevant quotations from the poem to complete the analysis on the right.

b Continue the paragraph, commenting on Cope's use of the **villanelle** form.

STUDENT

In 'Lonely Hearts', Cope makes those seeking partners sound desperate by using repetition, such as '_____'. The advertisements are all written to a formula, such as '_____', like they are in real life. Cope exaggerates the impossible demands people make, for example '_____ _____'. Cope makes clever use of irony as the advertisements unwittingly reveal the minus points, for example '_____'.

Writing with a persona

When poets use the first person, 'I', you cannot assume that they are speaking as themselves. They may be exploring what it is like to be someone else. This is called taking on a **persona**.

Carol-Ann Duffy wrote 'Stealing' after reading a newspaper article about a stolen snowman. The thief in her poem steals other items too, including a bust of Shakespeare. The poem is written from the thief's perspective.

ACTIVITY 6

a Look up 'Stealing' in your Anthology and read it aloud. What sounds are repeated throughout the poem? Back up your ideas with examples.

b How does Duffy make the thief sound sinister? Justify your ideas with quotations.

c Does Duffy create sympathy for this person and if so how? Consider the way she suggests that the thief feels like a failure.

d Does the poem reveal **why** the thief steals?

In the poem 'Mrs Lazarus', Duffy speaks as the wife of a man whom Jesus raised from the dead. Duffy often adopts the viewpoint of people who are not usually considered important and therefore do not usually get to give their version of events. Most people treat the raising of Lazarus as a demonstration of Jesus's miraculous power, but Duffy thinks carefully about the practical implications for both Lazarus and his wife.

ACTIVITY 7

a Read the first three stanzas of 'Mrs Lazarus' in your Anthology. List the ways that Mrs Lazarus mourns her dead husband.

b Why is her wedding ring a 'zero'?

c How does the widow move on?

d What is Lazarus's attitude is to being resurrected?

e How does Duffy create a sense of horror?

f What happens next? Create a short role-play of the conversations that might take place after the events in the poem.

The theme of nature

Nature has long been a favourite theme in poetry. It surrounds us and yet we struggle to fully understand it. Although nature can be very beautiful, it can also be bleak and dangerous. Both Clarke and Heaney explore the darker side of nature in some of their poems.

In 'Cold Knap Lake', Clarke tells the story of how her mother gave a girl the kiss of life. Although the lake exists, Clarke cannot remember if she witnessed the incident herself or if she was just told about it.

Like Clarke's poem, Heaney's 'Death of a Naturalist' is about a memory. Heaney remembers how, as a boy, he was frightened of frogs, which he imagined were seeking revenge on him for all the tadpoles he had collected.

ACTIVITY 8

a Read 'Cold Knap Lake' in your Anthology and list the colours referred to. How do the colours help Clarke to contrast life and death?

b The metaphor of 'long green silk' makes nature sound beautiful. How does Clarke introduce the idea of danger?

ACTIVITY 9

a Read 'Death of a Naturalist' in your Anthology. On a copy, highlight all the negative words. What effect do these create?

b Heaney recreates the sound of the frogs with **onomatopoeia**, or words that sound like what they describe, like 'slap'. List all the examples that you can find. How does this add to the impact of the poem?

c Why do you think the poem is called 'Death of a Naturalist'?

Poetry and the wider world

Poets often have strong views about things that are happening around them.

Heaney's poem 'Punishment' is about an ancient corpse dug up from a peat bog. He sees similarities between the fate of the corpse and women who were punished by other women by being 'tarred and feathered' during the troubles in Northern Ireland.

ACTIVITY 10

Read 'Punishment' in your Anthology. Consider what feelings Heaney creates in the reader:

- towards the young girl
- towards himself.

An example of a student's response is given below. Try to expand and improve on it.

STUDENT

Heaney describes the body of a young girl who was hanged, using natural metaphors: 'a barked sapling'. This indicates her youth and the colour of the corpse. He engages our sympathy by addressing the girl halfway through, calling her 'little adulteress', yet knows he would not have dared to save her, just as he did nothing when he was a witness of reprisals.

Benjamin Zephaniah also uses his poetry to deal directly with sensitive topics. 'What Stephen Lawrence Has Taught Us' is about racism. Stephen Lawrence was an A-level student who was killed in a racist attack. His killers have never been punished, and the results of an inquiry in 1999 indicated that this was linked to racism within the police force. Mr Condon, mentioned in the last stanza, was the Chief of Police at the time.

ACTIVITY 11

Research the case of Stephen Lawrence and then re-read the poem 'What Stephen Lawrence Has Taught Us' in your Anthology. List the positive and negative outcomes of the case. For example, it raised awareness of racism within the police force (positive outcome); however, a young teenager lost his life (negative outcome).

LEARNING CHECKLIST

In this chapter you will learn to:

1 Respond with insight and imagination; select text detail to support interpretations.

2 Explain how the writer uses language, structure and form to present ideas, themes and settings.

AO1 & AO2

UNIT 4

How to approach an unseen poem

If you choose to answer the unseen poem question, you will need to show the same skills as when writing about a poem from the Anthology. You need to look at how language, structure and form support the meanings within the poem. You also need to back up your ideas and interpretations with close reference to the text. Remember, analysing unseen poetry is about more than just identifying literary devices! You always need to think about **why** a poet has chosen to use a particular technique and **how** it influences the reader.

In the exam, you should read the poem at least twice and think carefully about what the poet is saying and how he or she is saying it. Look at the annotations that have been added to the extract below.

implies a poem is a wild animal

imperative verb, tells reader to focus at start of stanzas

From 'How to Capture a Poem'
by Angela Topping

Look for one at midnight
on the dark side of a backlit angel
or in the space between a sigh
and a word. Winter trees, those
elegant ladies dressed in diamonds
and white fur, may hide another.

Look for the rhythm in the feet
of a waltzing couple one, two, three-ing
in an empty hall, or in the sound
of any heartbeat, the breath of a sleeper,
the bossy rattle of keyboards in offices,
the skittering of paper blown along.

You could find a whole line
incised into stone or scrawled on sky.
Words float on air in buses, are bandied
on street corners, overheard in pubs,
caught in the pages of books, sealed
behind tight lips, marshalled as weapons.

Supposing you can catch a poem,
it won't tell you all it knows. Its voice
is a whisper through a wall, a streak of silk
going by, the scratch of a ghost, the creaks
of a house at night, the sound of the earth
vibrating in spring, with all its secret life.

metaphor suggests the mysterious nature of poetry

onomatopoeia brings sounds to life

Practising annotation

Making notes around the poem is a good way to explore it. Add brief comments to the margins, including question marks for parts you don't understand. Circle words you like and imagery that you find particularly striking. Use these annotations to record your immediate impressions and make them personal to you. Annotations can be made during the exam and will help you to focus closely on the poem before you start writing about it.

ACTIVITY I

Read 'Latin Master' on the right.

a Add your own annotations to a copy of the poem.

b Highlight all the words that relate to the ancient Romans, who spoke the language that Simpson had to learn. What effect do these words have?

c What impression do you form of the teacher?

d Does the poet have any regrets about learning things that were beyond the knowledge of his parents?

'Latin Master'
by Matt Simpson

Thou didst betray me to a lingring book,
And wrap me in a gown.

With detentions, impositions, cuffs,
he practised his imperial rule
on 'idlers', occupying minds
with legions of the strictest words
footslogged into Liverpool
on a bellyful of ancient deaths.

He altered all our history,
until the sea
seemed to lose its dragging power
and we learnt to hate our dockland streets
and know ourselves barbarian.

His Latin verbs put me to work
inside the fort,
made turncoat of me in the end.

Even his kindness after four o'clock
when he cranked a wind-up gramophone
inviting in his blue-eyed boys
to share the spoils
of Bach cantatas, symphonies by Brahms,
lost us our purchase on the things of home,
made traitors of us to our kind.

Selecting quotations

When writing about poetry, it is important to provide evidence for your ideas. This evidence should be quotations from the poem. However, you do not need to include long quotations; short ones, even just single words, embedded in your own sentences can be very effective. Remember to comment on your chosen quotation and to link it back to the point you wish to make.

Below is part of a student's response to 'Latin Master'.

'Latin Master' is about a Latin teacher. The list of punishments: 'detentions, impositions, cuffs,' shows how strict he is. Yet he is kind to his favourites, playing them music after school. The boys are all from working-class families who live near dockyards but Latin changes them, just like the Romans changed Britain: 'we learnt to hate our dockland streets'. Simpson feels that he has been taken over to the enemy side: 'made turncoat of me'. The phrases: 'his imperial rule' and 'share the spoils' shows the invasion of the boys' minds as it takes place. The boys will no longer follow their fathers to sea but may go to university and pursue a different path in life. This is at once a betrayal and an opportunity.

Simpson's language reflects his working-class origins with words like 'bellyful' and 'foot-slogged', juxtaposed with his new-found knowledge of words derived from Latin, such as 'imperial', 'occupying', 'legions' and 'barbarian'. Simpson's poem is personal on one level, but many can relate to it because it is about the way people change as they grow up and leave behind familiar things.

ACTIVITY 2

With a partner, discuss how you might add to or improve this response. Look back at the poem and think about:

- the first two lines and the implication of the word 'betray'
- the description of the sea's 'dragging power'
- the use of the phrase 'our kind'.

Free verse

Free verse is a form of poetry which has no fixed pattern; it does not have a regular beat or a set rhyme scheme. This form gives the poet flexibility to use different line lengths, stanza breaks and internal rhymes. However, this flexibility does not mean that free verse is not highly crafted. Poets will still often use poetic devices, and the choice of every word and its position in the poem will still be very carefully thought-out. Both of the poems that you have worked on in this chapter so far are written in free verse.

Free verse is well-suited to conveying subtle and sombre tones because it is one of the closest poetic forms to conversation.

ACTIVITY 3

a Read the free verse poem 'Early in the Morning' by Li-Young Lee, on the right, and the annotations that accompany it.

b Add more annotations of your own to a copy of the poem.

c Comment on how Li-Young Lee creates sound patterns within the poem without using a fixed rhyme scheme.

'Early in the Morning'
by Li-Young Lee

delicate words used to set a quiet scene

While the long grain is softening
in the water, gurgling
over a low stove flame, before
the salted Winter Vegetable is sliced
for breakfast, before the birds,
my mother glides an ivory comb
through her hair, heavy
and black as calligrapher's ink.

simile suggests the beauty of her hair

She sits at the foot of the bed.
My father watches, listens for
the music of the comb
against hair.
My mother combs

run-on lines suggest fluidity

pulls her hair back
tight, rolls it
around two fingers, pins it
in a bun to the back of her head.
For half a hundred years she has done this.
My father likes to see it like this.
He says it is kempt.

But I know
it is because of the way
my mother's hair falls
when he pulls the pins out.
Easily, like the curtains
when they untie them in the evening.

line-break after 'heavy' accentuates the weight

line-break creates suspense

opposite of unkempt, his father's joke

simile shows the privacy and beauty of mature love

Annotations should be short and concise. You should keep the question in mind when you make them and use them to record your initial response to the poem. You can then develop your points fully in your written answer.

Using literary terms

Literary terms provide the vocabulary for commenting on language. They are part of a poet's toolbox. It is important that you understand literary terms and that you are confident about using them.

ACTIVITY 4

Below is a table to help you revise literary terms. You need to match each term on the right to the correct row in the table. The table gives an explanation of each device with examples and a description of its effects.

 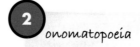

1 simile

2 onomatopoeia

3 rhyme

4 alliteration

5 tone

6 rhythm

7 pun

	EXPLANATION	EXAMPLES	EFFECTS
a	words that sound like the thing they describe	splash, bang, thud, whizz, screech, crack, crisp, flutter, scream	engages the reader's senses and makes descriptions more realistic
b	words beginning with the same letter	'dulls to distance all we are' 'my type-writer tapping under stars'	emphasizes words; can help create sound and rhythm in a poem or add to an overall mood
c	humorous use of a word which has more than one meaning	'having done that, Thou hast done' (In this quote, the poet John Donne, creates a pun on his own name)	shows a poet's cleverness; can make a point or amuse the reader; creates deeper layers of meaning
d	a similar sound in the endings of words	wealth – health (full rhyme)	can make a poem more memorable; adds to rhythm; can be used for emphasis
e	the beat in a poem; this can form different patterns	iambic, a pattern of an unstressed syllable followed by a stressed syllable	paces the text, makes it flow and can create different moods
f	how you would read a poem if you read out loud (its 'voice')	can be angry, serious, sad, jokey, quiet, conversational, etc.	adds to the mood and emotional power of the poem; a sudden shift can be used to shock the reader
g	a comparison between two things using 'like' or 'as'	'like a little dog, I followed her.'	helps you to see how a poet imagines things; can be used to convey emotions

Poems to discuss

Now you have the chance to consolidate the skills you have
developed and practised in this chapter.

ACTIVITY 4

Read the poems below. Discuss what you
like and what particularly interests you about
them. They both contain a great deal to make
you think, and present a different variation
of imagery, form and structure. In particular,
consider:

- what 'silence' comes to mean in the last
  line of the poem by Edward Lucie-Smith
- why Frost refers to the Garden of Eden in
  a nature poem.

'Silence'
by Edward Lucie-Smith

Silence: one would willingly
Consume it, eat it like bread.
There is never enough. Now
When we are silent, metal
Still rings upon shuddering
Metal; a door slams; a child
Cries; other lives around us.

But remember, there is no
Silence within; the belly
Sighs, grumbles, and what is that
Loud knocking, that summoning?
A drum beats, a drum beats. Hear
Your own noisy machine, which
Is moving towards silence.

'Nothing Gold Can Stay'
by Robert Frost

Nature's first green is gold,
Her hardest hue to hold.
Her early leaf's a flower;
But only so an hour.
Then leaf subsides to leaf.
So Eden sank to grief,
So dawn goes down to day.
Nothing gold can stay.

TRY THIS!

> A poem begins in delight and ends in wisdom.
>
> (Robert Frost)

What is a poem?

Consider these attempts to define poetry:

> Poetry… says heaven and earth in one word.
>
> (Christopher Fry)

> poetry is magic. It is a ll against insensitivity, ure of imagination, norance and barbarism.
>
> harles Causley)

> Every good poem, in fact, is a bridge built from the known, familiar side of life over into the unknown.
>
> (C. Day Lewis)

> Composition in verse or some comparable patterr arrangement of language in which the expression o feelings and ideas is given intensity by the use of distinctive style and rhyth.
>
> (Oxford English Dictionar

> Petry is the breath and finer spirit of all knowledge
>
> (William Wordsworth)

> Genuine poetry can communicate before it is understood.
>
> (T. S. Eliot)

> …the best words in the best order.
>
> (Samuel Taylor Coleridge)

ACTIVITY 1

How would you define poetry? Discuss your ideas with a partner and come up with your own definition.

Song writing

There is a strong link between poetry and song lyrics. Both poetry and songs tend to have strong rhythm and often rhyme. They are also usually best heard rather than read. Many early poems were sung to music played on a lyre (a small harp), which is they are referred to as 'lyrical poems'.

Thinking about poetry as song lyrics may help you to describe the tone of a poem. For example, an angry tone might be like a heavy metal song; a sad tone would be more like a soul ballad.

Artists

How to capture a poem
Latin Master

MENU

ACTIVITY 2

Discuss the poem on the right with a partner or in a small group.

- How is the poem similar to song lyrics?
- If this poem were a song, what type of song would it be?
- Try setting the poem to music and performing it for your class.
- Write your own poem or song about something you love.

EXTENSION TASK

Share your favourite poem with the class by making a slide show or video using video-editing software. Either recite the poem as a voice-over for the visual production or add suitable sound files. Show the finished production to the class.

'Coffee in Heaven'
by John Agard

You'll be greeted
by a nice cup of coffee
when you get to heaven
and strains of angelic harmony.

But wouldn't you be devastated
if they only serve decaffeinated
while from the percolators of hell

your soul was assaulted
by Satan's fresh espresso

What will I be assessed on in the exam?

When preparing for the exam, think carefully about the skills you will be assessed on. (See page 104 to remind yourself of the full wording of AO1 and AO2.)

What key aspects should I focus on?

Respond to texts with insight and imagination

This means that you need to show that you understand what a poem is about. You should explain what ideas the writer is putting forward and his or her point of view on the subject matter. Ask yourself questions about the poet's purpose. For example, is the poet trying to shock you into agreeing with his or her attitude to war? Is the poet trying to amuse you by treating his or her subject in a new and different way?

Select text detail to support interpretations

This means being able to back up your ideas with details from the poem. Examiners often remind you to do this, ending many poetry questions with 'Remember to refer closely to the words and phrases the poet uses'. Examiners cannot award very high marks if you do not support your ideas with evidence.

Language, structure and form

You will need to keep these aspects carefully in mind when you are preparing to write about poetry. Because poems are usually much shorter than plays and novels, poets need to choose their words with particular care. They also need to think carefully about the structure and form of their poems, whether to use rhyme and/or rhythm, or write in sonnet form or ballad style, for example.

EXAMINER'S TIPS

You can gain marks in your exam by identifying the effects of literary devices in the poem. If you find a metaphor, an oxymoron, alliteration, assonance or any other literary device in a poem, always try to show what it adds to the poem.

Reading poems

The more poems you read, the more you will develop your understanding of the way the poets use language and the effects they want to create. Whether you plan to write about one of the set poets in the Anthology or to tackle the unseen poem, it is worth taking the time to read all the poems in your Anthology. Not, of course, all in one go, but perhaps one a week. Think about what you've read and why you enjoyed, or did not enjoy, each poem.

Writing about a poem in the exam

If you're studying 15 poems by one poet in your Anthology, **do study them all carefully**. Don't risk only studying half of them and hoping that one of those will turn up in the exam, as it is very possible that the questions will turn out to be on the half you haven't studied!

Structuring your answer

It's worth having a basic structure to follow when writing about a poem. Examiners are sometimes surprised when an answer begins with a long paragraph about some detail or style of the poem; for example, rhyming patterns, when there has been no introduction or indication of what the poem is actually about.

Here is one possible structure you might find helpful to follow:

Oh no!

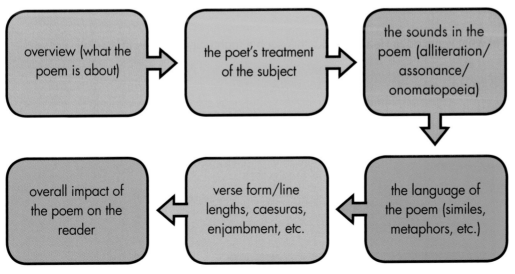

overview (what the poem is about) → the poet's treatment of the subject → the sounds in the poem (alliteration/ assonance/ onomatopoeia) → the language of the poem (similes, metaphors, etc.) → verse form/line lengths, caesuras, enjambment, etc. → overall impact of the poem on the reader

SEAMUS HEANEY: Death of a Naturalist

All year the flax-dam festered in the heart
Of the townland; green and heavy headed
Flax had rotted there, weighted down by huge sods.
Daily it sweltered in the punishing sun.
Bubbles gargled delicately, bluebottles   5
Wove a strong gauze of sound around the smell.
There were dragon-flies, spotted butterflies,
But best of all was the warm thick slobber
Of frogspawn that grew like clotted water
In the shade of the banks. Here, every spring   10
I would fill jampotfuls of the jellied
Specks to range on window-sills at home,
On shelves at school, and wait and watch until
The fattening dots burst into nimble-
Swimming tadpoles. Miss Walls would tell us how   15
The daddy frog was called a bullfrog
And how he croaked and how the mammy frog

Laid hundreds of little eggs and this was
Frogspawn. You could tell the weather by frogs too   20
For they were yellow in the sun and brown
In rain.

Then one hot day when fields were rank
With cowdung in the grass the angry frogs
Invaded the flax-dam; I ducked through hedges   25
To a coarse croaking that I had not heard
Before. The air was thick with a bass chorus.
Right down the dam gross-bellied frogs were cocked
On sods; their loose necks pulsed like sails. Some hopped:
The slap and plop were obscene threats. Some sat   30
Poised like mud grenades, their blunt heads farting.
I sickened, turned, and ran. The great slime kings
Were gathered there for vengeance and I knew
That if I dipped my hand the spawn would clutch it.

Sample task 4.3

1a   In what ways does Heaney make this such a frightening experience?   [16]

UNIT 4

Student response 4.3

In 'Death of a Naturalist', Heaney presents an experience so frightening that the developing 'naturalist' in the poem, a child, undergoes a metaphorical 'death', suggesting that his terror has killed his curiosity about nature. He senses that the 'great slime kings' have come to the flax-dam for 'vengeance', punishing the child for his crime of stealing their spawn. The descriptions of the flax-dam at the beginning of the poem and the 'gross-bellied frogs' at the end are particularly effective in creating a frightening atmosphere.

The most frightening part for the child comes towards the end of the poem. However, there is a disquietingly ominous quality about the flax-dam in the opening lines. Throughout much of the poem Heaney uses sounds and smells to create an atmosphere likely to frighten a child. The alliteration of 'flax-dam festered' puts emphasis on the unpleasant word 'festered' that suggests infection (picked up in 'rotted' in line 3) and the alliteration and assonance of 'heavy headed' suggest heat and oppression, inflicted by 'the punishing sun'. The 'gauze' of sound woven by the bluebottles continues the pattern of infection and disease imagery as they seem to be bandaging up the foul smell. Even before the frogs invade, the flax-dam is a frightening place, though not sufficiently so to keep the child from collecting the frogspawn. However, the description of the frogspawn is ominous: 'warm thick slobber' suggests drooling, and the simile comparing it to 'clotted water' makes it seem thick and sticky.

The atmosphere becomes less intense in Miss Walls' classroom where the teacher gives the class a brief introduction to the facts of life. Far from frightening, the frogs here have become 'daddy frog' and 'mammy frog' making their transformation into

immediately addresses the question

clear overview of poem

skilful weaving in of quotations

identifies the crescendo of horror

confident use of technical terms

clear analysis of effects

understands the structure of the poem and varying tension

'great slime kings' both unexpected and still more frightening.

When the child returns to the flax-dam, Heaney uses military imagery. Like an army, the frogs have 'invaded'; like guns, they are 'cocked'. Heaney uses the simile 'Poised like mud grenades' to suggest that the child is in immediate and deadly danger. Unpleasant smells have returned: the fields are 'rank' and foul-smelling. Heaney uses sounds to make the experience more vivid and frightening. The alliteration of 'coarse croaking' imitates the hard sounds of the frogs. The onomatopoeia of the two monosyllables 'slap' and 'plop' creates unpleasant noises, and the 'farting heads' reinforces the atmosphere of frightening, disgusting sounds and smells. 'Coarse' is a very appropriate word to describe the sounds and smells of the flax-dam and its occupying army.

Kings are defied at one's peril, even if they are kings only of repulsive slime. The way Heaney describes the child's experience at the flax-dam makes clear why the naturalist in him died.

consistent reference to the question

good analysis of language evoking sounds and smells

EXAMINER'S TIPS

Remember to look very closely at the **language** poets use. When referring to particular techniques that are used, explain how they have an effect on the reader, or contribute to the overall meaning of the poem.

EXAMINER'S COMMENTS OCR
RECOGNISING ACHIEVEMENT

- This response is well-focused and its discussion of language is succinct and sophisticated.

- Excellent use of technical terms and clear understanding of literary effects.

- This is a strong response that would be placed in the top band.

FOUNDATION TIER

Source text 4.4   **BENJAMIN ZEPHANIAH: Three Black Males**

Three black males get arrested
When they said they seek two whites,
Dis poet said that's expected
For we have no human rights,
We die in their police stations   5
We do nothing to get caught
We are only in white nations
When we win them gold in sports.

Three black males in the system
So the system just rolls on.   10
Can you recognise the victims
When the truth is dead and gone,
Can you recognise their anguish
When they beg you time to care
Or do you forget your language   15
When three black males disappear?

Raphael Rowe is not an angel
And Michael Davis ain't
Let us be straight and factual
Randolph Johnson is no saint,   20
The Home Office has a God complex
But that office is not great
For it does not recognise subtext
Injustice or mistakes.

Let all poets now bear witness   25
Let the storyteller tell
Let us deal with dis white business
Dis democracy's not well,
The cops, the judge and jury
Need some helping it does seem   30
And three black males with a story
Fight
So truth can reign supreme.

Sample task 4.4

1a What view of racial issues does Zephaniah powerfully convey to you
   in 'Three Black Males'?

You should consider:

- references to injustice in the poem

- the poet's feelings towards the men the poem

- The words and phrases the poet uses.   *[10]*

'Three Black Males' is a poem about three men who were called the M25 Three, because they were found guilty of carrying out crimes around the M25 motorway in 1998 and were sentenced to prison for life. They appealed and were set free in the year 2000. Some of the victims said they were certain that at least one of their attackers or perhaps even two were white. The M25 Three were Raphael Rowe, Michael Davis and Randolph Johnson as Benjamin Zephaniah tells us their names in the third verse. The title of the poem says that the three people who were arrested were black so the poet is telling us they must have been victims of racial prejudice.

The poet says that this happened because they do not have 'human rights'. The poet must know what he is talking because he is black. He talks about how black males die in police stations, but as the M25 Three were set free in the year 2000, they couldn't have died. The poet says that black people are only accepted in white nations when they can win gold medals for that nation in sports and then the white nations are proud of them.

Then he says when black men are 'in the system', which means when they are in prison, people haven't time to care about them and don't speak up for their human rights. Then he says that the three men weren't angels. I know that they all had criminal records and that's probably the reason they were found guilty as the jury must have thought they were hardened

shows background knowledge

understands the racial issue

knows the poet is black himself

shows understanding of poet's point

Student response 4.4 continued

good focus on language

criminals. In the last verse the poet says 'Let us deal with dis white business' which means the business of race and how it is important that 'truth can reign supreme'.

The words and phrases the poet uses are easy to understand. He uses 'dis' instead of 'this' because this is probably the language he and the three black males use. In the last verse he says that the judge and jury 'Need some helping it does seem'. By using their language he shows he's on their side. He is also a 'performance poet' so he reads his poems aloud to audiences. The second to last line of the poem just has the one word 'Fight' to make it stand out.

'Three Black Males' shows that racism is wrong and we must fight against it.

good use of quotations, but need to go into more depth

points out effect of structure

EXAMINER'S COMMENTS

- This response shows some understanding of the poem and comments on some aspects of the language and structure.

- It shows background knowledge but does not focus enough on the detail of the poem; for example, the repeated use of 'we' and 'let'; the powerful opening line; vocabulary such as 'beg' and 'anguish'; the appeal to 'you' in verse 2 and the use of rhythm and rhyme.

- This response would fall into the lower band.

EXAMINER'S TIPS

It's often a good idea to read poems **aloud** (although not in the exam room!). This will help you to fully appreciate the use of rhyme and rhythm in the poem as well as the poet's choice of tone.

Source text 4.5

UNSEEN POEM

ANDREW MOTION: Anne Frank Huis

Even now, after twice her lifetime of grief
and anger in the very place, whoever comes
to climb these narrow stairs, discovers how
the bookcase slides aside, then walks through
shadow into sunlit rooms, can never help   5

but break her secrecy again. Just listening
is a kind of guilt: the Westerkirk repeats
itself outside, as if all time worked round
towards her fear, and made each stroke
die down on guarded streets. Imagine it –   10

three years of whispering and loneliness
and plotting, day by day, the Allied line

in Europe with a yellow chalk. What hope
she had for ordinary love and interest
survives her here, displayed above the bed   15

as pictures of her family; some actors;
fashions chosen by Princess Elizabeth.
And those who stoop to see them find
not only patience missing its reward,
but one enduring wish for chances   20

like my own: to leave as simply
as I do, and walk at ease
up dusty tree-lined avenues, or watch
a silent barge come clear of bridges
settling their reflections in the blue canal.   25

Sample task 4.5

13 How does Andrew Motion make this poem about Anne Frank's house so moving?

You should consider:

- the description of the house
- what the poet hears
- what the poet imagines about Anne's life
- the poet's thoughts in the last verse
- some of the language the poet uses
- the structure of the poem
- anything else that you think is important.   [16]

Student response 4.5

a direct personal response to the question

I think this poem is very moving. The poet, Andrew Motion, helps me to understand how awful it must have been to live like Anne Frank did for two years and to ultimately get caught and sent to a concentration camp.

The poet describes the house very effectively. He says that the stairs were 'narrow' so she must have had little room to go up and down them, and she must have had to hide in a room that was hidden by bookcases. The room was at least sunny, so it must have had upstairs windows. Perhaps she had to live in an attic.

understands the sense of restriction

perceptive conclusion

I think the poet sees himself as a visitor to the house, who is disturbing something, like Anne's need to be secret within the house. He puts himself in Anne's place and can hear the clock that she heard when she was hiding. I think it is moving when he says the Westerkirk, which I think is some sort of clock as it makes strokes, somehow times her fear. He brings the reader into the poem when he says 'Imagine it' and he implies that she must have been lonely. I think it is sad that she must have been 'plotting'. She must have been planning to get away or perhaps be rescued as she is following the 'Allied line' which is perhaps coming towards her, like a rescue line. I think the poet makes her moving to the reader, as she seems like a normal girl. She put pictures of her family on the wall, and some actors, as we put up posters of actors and pop stars. She must have hoped to live a normal life.

direct link to the question

understands effect of poet's technique

personal response and apt comparison

Student response 4.5 continued

good weaving in of quotations

The last verse is very moving because the poet talks about how he can leave the house 'simply' and enjoy the view of the streets and the 'blue canal'. All the things that Anne Frank could not do. The poet uses words that encourage the reader to feel sympathy for Anne. She felt 'grief and anger' as well as 'fear'. The poet begins by climbing the stairs to the offices, and seems to breathe a sigh of relief when he gets away from the house. The last verse is very peaceful with words like 'clear' and 'blue'. It is moving that the poet is happy to come back to a life where you do not have to hide.

sensitive interpretation

EXAMINER'S COMMENTS OCR

RECOGNISING ACHIEVEMENT

- This is a strong response which uses apt quotations to support the ideas expressed.

- It shows a sensitive appreciation of Anne's situation and the poet's response to it.

- For higher marks, the student needs to look more closely at the language the poet uses. For example, 'grief and anger', 'guarded streets', 'survives' and 'silent barge'. Why is the language so short of similes and metaphors? Is there anything to be said about the structure of the verses, each consisting of five lines and each running into each other?

- As it stands, this is an upper-band response.

Source text 4.6

UNSEEN POEM

TONY HARRISON: An Old Score

Capless, conscious of the cold patch on my head
where my father's genes have made me almost bald
I walk along the street where he dropped dead,
my hair cut his length now, although I'm called
poet, in my passport.   5
                        When it touched my ears
he dubbed me *Paganinny** and it hurt.
I did then, and do now, choke back my tears –

Wi' 'air like that you ought to wear a skirt!

If I'd got a violin for every day   10
he'd said *weer's thi fiddle?* at my flowing hair
I'd have a whole string orchestra to play
romantic background as once more I'm there
where we went for my forced fortnightly clip
now under new, less shearing, ownership,   15
And in the end it's that that makes me cry –

JOE'S SALOON'S become KURL UP & DYE,

*the father calls his son Paganinny after Paganini, the famous violinist

Sample task 4.6

13 What feelings about his father does the poet convey to you in this poem?

You should consider:

- the poet's relationship with his father when he was young
- the way his father spoke to him
- the way he describes his hair and how it was cut
- his hair now
- what makes the poet cry
- the words and phrases the poet uses
- anything else in the poem that you think is important. [10]

Student response 4.6

shows some awareness of key idea

The poet's relationship with his father when he was young wasn't very good as his father seemed to tease him a lot about how long his hair was. It reached his ears and he says that he felt hurt when his father called him 'Paganinny'. He says that he 'ought to wear a skirt' so he is calling him a girl and this makes the poet nearly cry. It hurt him so much that he nearly cries when he thinks about it when he's grown up. I think what his father said was embarrassing. He also kept saying 'weer's thi fiddle' and that must have been annoying. He says he went for a 'clip' every fortnight and that makes him cry when he thinks about it. Where he went for a hair cut has changed its name and seems to have become trendy.

understands how the young boy felt

misses the point about the pun die/dye

EXAMINER'S TIPS

Read as many contemporary poems from the Anthology as you can. This will help you to develop your poetry-reading skills.

Student response 4.6 continued

The writer doesn't have long hair now as he is 'almost bald'. His father dropped dead in the street. I think he misses his father as he talks about crying, even though his father must have been annoying. The way the father spoke was also annoying as he spoke badly and incorrectly. The poet doesn't talk like that so the way his father talked must have been embarrassing. I think the father made the poet interested in music as he seems to play every day on a violin.

There is rhyme in this poem. It is ABABCDCD in the first part, but there is a short line where the word passport doesn't rhyme with anything. The rhyme helps the poem to flow.

This poem makes me happy that my father is not an annoying person.

perceptive comment

this is incorrect; the student has misread the poem

reference to rhyme scheme unhelpful and doesn't relate to question

EXAMINER'S COMMENTS OCR☆
RECOGNISING ACHIEVEMENT

- This answer shows some awareness of key ideas.
- Some effective use of short quotation.
- There is not enough detailed focus; for example, on the dialect of the father; the references to music; the image of sheep shearing; the language and structure of the poem.
- This response would be placed in the lower band.

OXFORD
UNIVERSITY PRESS

Great Clarendon Street, Oxford OX2 6DP

Oxford University Press is a department of the University of Oxford.
It furthers the University's objective of excellence in research,
scholarship, and education by publishing worldwide in

Oxford   New York

Auckland   Cape Town   Dar es Salaam   Hong Kong   Karachi
Kuala Lumpur   Madrid   Melbourne   Mexico City   Nairobi
New Delhi   Shanghai   Taipei   Toronto

With offices in

Argentina   Austria   Brazil   Chile   Czech Republic   France   Greece
Guatemala   Hungary   Italy   Japan   Poland   Portugal   Singapore
South Korea   Switzerland   Thailand   Turkey   Ukraine   Vietnam

Oxford is a registered trade mark of Oxford University Press
in the UK and in certain other countries

© Oxford University Press 2010

Authors: D.C. Coleman, Annie Fox, Garrett O'Doherty, Angela Topping,
Carmel Waldron

The moral rights of the authors have been asserted

Database right Oxford University Press (maker)

First published 2010

British Library Cataloguing in Publication Data

Data available

ISBN 978-0-19-832945-9

10 9 8 7 6 5 4 3 2 1

Printed in Spain by Cayfosa-Impresia Ibérica

Paper used in the production of this book is a natural, recyclable product made
from wood grown in sustainable forests. The manufacturing process conforms to
the environmental regulations of the country of origin.

Acknowledgements

The publisher and authors would like to thank the following for their permission
to reproduce photographs and other copyright material:
p10: Donald Cooper/Photostage; **p11**: Alastair Muir/Rex Features; **p12**: Kean
Collection/Staff/Hulton Archive/Getty Images; **p14t**: Creatas/Photolibrary;
p14b: Roman Sigaev/Shutterstock; **p16**: Everett Collection/Rex Features; **p17**:
Buena Vista/Everett/Rex Features; **p18l**: 20thC.Fox/Everett/Rex Features; **p18r**:
themoviestorecollection.com; **p19t**: Robbie Jack/Corbis; **p19b**: Sonypics/Everett/
Rex Features; **p21t**: The Everett Collection/Rex Features; **p21m**: Columbia/The
Kobal Collection; **p21b**: The Ronald Grant Archive; **p22t**: Sony Pics/Everett/Rex
Features; **p22b**: c.Sony Pics/Everett/Rex Features; **p24-25**: javarman/Shutterstock;
p33: Ronfromyor/Stockxpert; **p34**: First World War Poetry Digital Archive;
p35t: Javarman/Shutterstock; **p35m**: Alphaspirit/Shutterstock; **p35b**: Sundeep
Goel/Shutterstock; **p36t**: Archive Photos/Stringer/Hulton Archive/Getty Images;
p36m: Ellesmere Manuscript,facsimile edition, 1911,English School,(15th
century) (after)/Private Collection/The Bridgeman Art Library; **p37**: Andrew Park/
Shutterstock; **p39**: Fine Art Photographic Library/Corbis; **p40**: Lebrecht Music &
Arts Photo Library/Photolibrary; **p41**: Mary Evans Picture Library/Photolibrary;
p43: Rothenstein,Sir William(1872-1945) /Private Collection/Whitford &
Hughes,London,UK /The Bridgeman Art Library; **p44**: Lebrecht Music & Arts
Photo Library/Photolibrary; **p54**: Donald Cooper/Photostage; **p57**: Acorn Pictures
Ltd/The Kobal Collection; **p58**: Alastair Muir/Rex Features; **p59**: Acorn Pictures
Ltd/The Kobal Collection; **p60t**: wessley/Shutterstock; **p60b**: acequestions/
Shutterstock; **p61t**: BBC Photo Library; **p61m**: Claudia Gabriela Tapuleasa/Big
Stock Photo; **p61b**: Brian Jackson/Big Stock Photo; **p62**: Photo © Michal Daniel,
2008; **p63t**: Photo © Michal Daniel, 2008; **p63b**: Arts Decoratifs,Paris,France/
Archives Charmet /The Bridgeman Art Library; **p64**: Fox Searchlight/The Kobal
Collection; **p66t**: FPG/Staff/The Hulton Archive/Getty Images; **p66m**: Underwood
& Underwood/Corbis; **p66b**: The Mariners' Museum/Corbis; **p67t**: Paul Lovelace/
Rex Features; **p67b**: Dixon,Henry (1820-1892)/S.P.R.O.L. Collection/City of
London; **p79**: BBC Films/Film Council/The Kobal Collection; **p80**: Orientaly/
Shutterstock; **p82**: Ronald Grant Archive; **p84t**: Alain Nogues/Sygma/Corbis;
p84b: Miramax/Everett/Rex Features; **p85t**: Miramax/Everett/Rex Features;
p85b: Radu Sigheti/Reuters; **p86t**: Courtesy of the National Library of Ireland;
p86b: Ronald Grant Archive; **p90t**: Carly Rose Hennigan/Shutterstock; **p90b**:
Image Source/OUP; **p91t**: Universal/The Kobal Collection; **p91b**: David Turnley/
Corbis; **p92**: Mark Winfrey/Shutterstock; **p93**: Miramax/Everett/Rex Features;
p94: Sandra Cunningham/Shutterstock; **p94l**: The Ronald Grant Archive;
p94m: The Ronald Grant Archive; **p94r**: The Ronald Grant Archive; **p95**:
Janaka Dharmasena/Shutterstock; **p95t**: Everett Collection/Rex Features;
p95m: James Steidl/Shutterstock; **p106**: Capital Pictures; **p107t**: Working
Title/The Kobal Collection; **p107b**: Ronald Grant Archive; **p108t**: LiveMan/
Shutterstock; **p108b**: Gladskikh Tatiana/Shutterstock; **p109**: Gillespaire/
Dreamstime; **p110**: Sami Sarkis/Photolibrary; **p111**: The Halas and Batchelor
Collection; **p113**: Ronald Grant Archive; **p115**: Lebrecht Music & Arts Photo
Library/Photolibrary; **p116**: Photodisc/OUP; **p117**: Corel/OUP; **p118t**: The
Halas and Batchelor Collection; **p118b**: The Halas and Batchelor Collection;
p119l: c.Focus/Everett/Rex Features; **p119r**: Corel/OUP; **p130**: Tischenko Irina/
Shutterstock; **p131t**: Anthony Blake/Photolibrary; **p131b**: Benis Arapovic/
Dreamstime; **p133**: OUP; **p134t**: Alexandra Borsuk/Fotolia; **p134m**: Robert
Byron/Dreamstime; **p134b**: Seen/Fotolia; **p135**: Rex Features; **p137t**: Susannah
Ireland/Rex Features: **p137b**: Ferran Paredes/Reuters; **p138b**: Ian O'Leary/
Photolibrary; **p140l**: Henry Diltz/Corbis; **p140r**: Oxford Scientific/Photolibrary;
p141: Richard Ashworth/Photolibrary; **p143m**: The Art Archive/H.M. Herget/
NGS Image Collection; **p143bl**: Morgan Lane Photography/Shutterstock;
p143br: Serbin Dmitry/Shutterstock; **p144l**: Victor Zastol'skiy/Fotolia; **p145**:
Nana Kelley/Big Stock Photo; **p147**: Djun/Dreamstime; **p148**: Apple Inc.

Illustrations by Flora Douville, Oxford Designers & Illustrators, Rheannon
Cummins, Theresa Tibbetts, Tom Genower. Cover illustration: Sian Thomas

The publisher and authors are grateful for permission to reprint the following
copyright material:
John Agard: 'Coffee in Heaven', copyright © John Agard 1997, from *Alternative
Anthem: Selected Poems* (Bloodaxe, 2009), reprinted by permission of Bloodaxe
Books; **Alan Bennett**: extracts from *The History Boys* (Faber, 2004), reprinted
by permission of Faber & Faber Ltd.; **Roddy Doyle**: extract from *Paddy Clarke
Ha Ha Ha* (Secker & Warburg, 1993), reprinted by permission of the Random
House Group Ltd.; **Robert Frost**: 'Nothing Gold can Stay' from *The Poetry of
Robert Frost* edited by Edward Connery Lathem (Jonathan Cape, 1971), reprinted
by permission of the Random House Group Ltd.; **Athol Fugard**: extracts from
Tsotsi (Canongate, 2009), originally published by Ad Donker, South Africa 1980,
reprinted by permission of Canongate Books and William Morris Endeavour
Entertainment for the author.; **William Golding**: extracts from *Lord of
the Flies* (Faber, 1954), reprinted by permission of Faber & Faber Ltd.; **Tony
Harrison**: 'An Old Score' from *Collected Poems* (Penguin, 2007), reprinted by
permission of Gordon Dickerson for the author.; **Seamus Heaney**: 'Blackberry
Picking' and 'Death of a Naturalist' from *Death of a Naturalist* (Faber, 1966),
reprinted by permission of Faber & Faber Ltd.; **Harper Lee**: extracts from *To
Kill a Mockingbird* (Wm Heinemann 1960/Vintage 2004), copyright © Harper
Lee, reprinted by permission of the Random House Group Ltd, and Aitken
Alexander Associates.; **Li-Young Lee**: 'Early in the Morning' from *Rose: poems*
(Boa Editions, 1986), copyright © Li-Young Lee, reprinted by permission of
Boa Editions Ltd, www.boaeditions.org.; **Edward Lucie-Smith**: 'Silence' from
Changing Shape (Carcanet, 2002), reprinted by permission of Carcanet Press Ltd.;
Andrew Motion: 'Anne Frank Huis' from *Selected Poems 1976-1997* (Faber,
1998), reprinted by permission of Faber & Faber Ltd.; **George Orwell**: extracts
from *Animal Farm* (Penguin Modern Classics, 1972), copyright © George Orwell
1945, reprinted by permission of Bill Hamilton as the Literary Executor of
the Estate of the late Sonia Brownell Orwell and Secker & Warburg Ltd, c/o A
M Heath & Co Ltd.; **J B Priestley**: extract from *An Inspector Calls* (Heinemann
Plays, 1992), copyright © J B Priestley 1947, 1992, reprinted by permission of
PFD (www.pfd.co.uk) on behalf of The Estate of J B Priestley.; **Willy Russell**:
extracts from *Educating Rita* (Methuen Drama, 2007), copyright © Willy
Russell 1985, reprinted by permission of Methuen Drama, an imprint of A &
C Black Publishers. All rights whatsoever in this play are strictly reserved and
application for performance, etc. must be made before rehearsal to Casarotto
Ramsay & Associates Ltd, 7-12 Noel Street, London W1F 8GQ. No performance
may be given unless a licence has been obtained.; **Matt Simpson**: 'Latin
Master' from *Elegy for the Galosherman: New and Selected Poems* (Bloodaxe, 1990),
reprinted by permission of the heirs of Matt Simpson.; **Meera Syal**: extracts
from *Anita and Me* (Flamingo, 1997), copyright © Meera Syal 1996, reprinted by
permission of HarperCollins Publishers.; **Angela Topping**: lines from 'How to
Capture a Poem' from *Troubles Swapped for Something Fresh* (Salt, 2009), reprinted
by permission of the author.; **Benjamin Zephaniah**: 'Three Black Males'
from *Too Black, Too Strong* (Bloodaxe, 2003), reprinted by permission of Bloodaxe
Books.

Although we have made every effort to trace and contact all copyright holders
before publication this has not been possible in all cases. If notified, the
publisher will rectify any errors or omissions at the earliest opportunity.